HELP WITH ANXIETY

MOVING FROM SELF-WORRY TO SELF-LOVE

JENNIFER KYNDNES

CONTENTS

INTRODUCTION

Life is not only challenging at times—it can outright suck. As in, it will suck the life and vitality from both yourself and everyone around you, especially if you refuse to take responsibility for the things you have control over or even acknowledge you feel a certain way. These suppressed emotions and lack of action to deal with them can affect those around you. It's funny how one person can bring down the atmosphere of a room. Or, they can lift it up, leaving everyone in a bright and cheery mood.

We spread things. Not just germs, but our emotions, positive or negative, as well. And just as we can wash our hands and cover our mouths when we cough to help prevent spreading physical illness, we can use various methods, personal realization, and self-control to help clear our minds of the negative, unhealthy thoughts that have infected our minds and emotions and prevent them from latching onto those around us.

I've battled anxiety for as long as I can remember. It ate at my confidence and personal strength and I allowed myself to believe I was at the mercy of an uncaring world whose circumstances seemed bent on keeping me on unstable footing. I wish I could say

I am alone in this, but anxiety is becoming all too common, affecting an increasing number of adults that seems to be quickly growing out of control (Anxiety and Depression Association of America, 2020) leaving many individuals with the perception that they are powerless against anxiety and the often accompanying depression that afflicts them. Anxiety seems to have seeded itself into our lives, growing roots that when torn free can leave us reeling from the damage.

The damage can be magnified by those whose own fears and anxiety lead them to an unsavory and unloving reaction. This is why the sooner you recognize it within yourself, the sooner you can cut off this unhelpful and damaging cycle. And while it can be easier to regain control early on, most of those who suffer from long-term anxiety can still be empowered to excise it from their lives in gentle ways that will lead to healing. There is a way to reclaim your life. And while life contains a natural sense of anxiety from time to time, using this book to better understand yourself and work towards a healthy mindset will help you not only feel more at peace, it can also increase the quality of your life and help you gain a sense of satisfaction, accomplishment, and gratitude.

My journey to a healthier mental and emotional life free of uncontrolled anxiety was not a smooth one. I say "uncontrolled" because anxiety in and of itself can be used positively and we'll discuss that more later. I lived in fear of the "what-ifs." "What if my husband got into an accident on the way home?!" when he was barely five minutes late or "What if my friends actually think I am annoying?!" when I did not hear from someone as quickly as I would like. These are only a couple examples of the constant questioning that flitted through my mind and it caused this constant emotional certainty that assured me something was bound to go wrong. That I was hated or a bad mother. Because of my ever-increasing fears, I could not engage in most activities without experiencing the "worried response." In fact, if I learned something important was coming up on the weekend, the rest of my work week would be colored in panicked scenarios that entered and twisted my mind and took over my rational thinking.

It persisted to the point that every single week was just a constant feeling of nervousness and choking fear. I could not stop fretting over what was going to happen next. Worse, I was also thinking about what was *not* going to happen. All the while, my anxious whirlwind was affecting everyone around me in ways I could never have anticipated until one day I realized how much my children were struggling with going to school.

The reality of how I was affecting my children was brought to hideous life when my son stated, "I don't like myself, mom. Everything is just too hard. There is no point in being here." My heart was shattered and a dark realization spread through me. At the time, it was a hideous wound to both my heart and ego, but now I realize it was a necessary incident, albeit incredibly difficult, that helped me see how my internal life and constant anxiety were causing my children to pick up on it and internalize it as their own reality.

Sometimes, in order for us to make a change for the better, we must be forced to see how it is affecting the ones that matter the most to us. When my son's words stung my ears and my pride, I understood I had to stop living my life in fear. I know you may have heard you must "do it for yourself" when making changes in your life, but I don't think that is necessarily true. For me, I had to start with doing it for them—for my children. And to do that, I had to face the fact I was more engaged with these "what-ifs" and unnecessary fear than I was being aware of what my children were suffering from.

This allowed me to begin taking responsibility for my life. Instead of allowing life to happen to me, I needed to actively guide my life in the direction I wanted it to go. What really fascinates me about my own journey was just how easy it was to start changing my mindset from one of worries and "what-ifs" to one of self-control and gratitude. And gratitude, you will learn, is key to living your life to the fullest.

ONE STEP AT A TIME

I know you've heard this before, but life is all about the steps you take and you can only take them one at a time. That is a beautiful blessing, even if you may not yet know this. But, that is how you begin. That first step taking you to the next one. Eventually, you take enough steps toward the direction you want to go and a mile has passed you by. Progress has been made.

Best of all, it does not matter how slowly or quickly you get there. Life is full of steps and different stops along the way. Some will carry you to places you know you must escape from, and living with daily anxiety for the sake of worrying over "what-ifs" is one of them. It's a stop in the travels of your life you can learn not to get off at. Think of your journey like a bus you take. You can choose the route, which stops to get off at, and when it's time to switch buses altogether.

SWITCHING FROM THE ANXIETY ROUTE TO THE GRATEFUL ROUTE

It sounds so simple and easy to turn your life around the way some people talk. You may have been told to "just snap out of it!" or treated as if you could just pull a switch and the anxiety will just go away. What if I were to tell you that you could actually switch it off? That you really can reach out and flip the anxiety switch at will. Sounds crazy?

It's not wishful thinking. The trick is not turning the switch to the "off position," though. You are flipping it from "anxiety" to "self-love." Or, perhaps the best word is "gratefulness." It is my firm belief that overcoming anxiety and other emotionally debilitating experiences starts with willfully searching out the things in your life to be grateful for.

Before we get into how to build a life of gratitude, we are going to take a mental walk through the dangers of allowing anxiety to have the front seat in your life. If you feel trapped and desperate to be free, know that you truly are not alone in this. This book will help you to no longer be a passenger of your thoughts and feelings as well as start a journey of self-discovery that will lead to a healthy love of yourself. And when you love who you are, you can be the inspiration to help others do the same. And what could be better than building others up into the best versions of themselves after you've done it in your own life?

FEEDING FRENZY

Each of us has a story to tell about how anxiety affected us. Each chapter, including this one, will cover a short story about someone who lived with anxiety to the point that it crippled them in some area of their life. Just as my own story in the introduction, this one comes from a woman who suffered from constantly worrying about the things that could go wrong. Like me, even the occurrence of her husband being a few minutes late from work would have her fretting and wondering if he had died. Sometimes, she found herself thinking about the next steps and what she would need to do. Or, worse yet, she would dread she and the kids would be out on the streets.

The following will be in the words of our friend. To keep her privacy, we will call this woman "Alison," and this is her story:

I've always been a positive person. Personally, I never did understand where these thoughts came from. They would invade my thoughts suddenly, and instead of ignoring them, as I now know I should, I would entertain them. Because I have a very vivid imagination, I could literally picture these horrific scenarios of the people I loved most coming to bodily harm.

Worse, I could feel the emotions associated with their loss creep up on me. It's one thing to cry during a film, quite another to be wracked with emotional turmoil by a vision that overcame you so completely it felt as if it was real. My anxiety over something happening to others became so bad it began to interfere with my sleep. It wasn't just the nightmares. Well, maybe that was part of it. But I had great difficulty falling asleep, much less staying asleep, when I finally did.

Those nights I could hear and feel my heart thumping in my chest. I just could not stop thinking about all the things that could happen and go wrong. My thoughts were circular in that they fed on themselves, ensuring they were kept alive. I lived like this for years. Honestly, it was more like decades, as I am no longer a young woman.

Then, I discovered apps. You know, those things you can download onto your phone. There are so many it's hard to choose just one, but I went through several until I found one that worked best for me. Even then, I am constantly adjusting the one I am currently using. Oh! I should probably tell you what apps, I mean, shouldn't I?

The most obvious one I started with was one called "Calm," which is an app that helps with sleep, meditation, and relaxation. It's a nice app, and I know it works well for others, but for me, it did not quite fit my needs. However, it did help me understand how to be "in the moment" and to build myself up in positive ways by taking action. In the end, I started using a newer app, at least new to me, called Fabulous. This app helps you plan your day by splitting your "to-do list" across your day: morning, afternoon, and evening. Sometimes, I see it called "The fabulous," but I do not really care what it is officially called. All I know is that it really is fabulous, and it's made such a huge difference in my life.

The thing about apps and whether or not they work is whether or not you actually use them. You, and you alone, are responsible for opening them each day and following through. If it's not a good fit or you are simply not ready to take ownership of your own life, the app you choose will not be beneficial, in my opinion. Even the best app is useless if you don't open it up and keep at it.

What helps me stay on track is keeping my goals simple. At first, I wanted to just dump everything I wanted to accomplish into the app and get started right away. I was barely crawling and making goals to run a 5K the next morning. Let me tell you this: I did not run that 5K very much. So, I decided to start smaller. Much, much smaller.

So, I started going for a short walk. I did not worry about timing or speed. I just walked around my block. Sadly, some days had poor weather or were simply too hot. It was easy for me not to go for that damn walk. If you are wondering what walking has to do with anxiety, let me tell you that not walking caused my anxiety to skyrocket because I knew, deep inside, I was allowing something easily done to not happen.

I cannot tell you precisely when it started, but I had taken on the habit of praying while still in bed and when I went to bed for the night. I understand prayer is not for everyone, but for me, I focused on the things I was grateful for. I would thank God for waking me up to a new day. I would thank him for the roof over my head. I would express my thankfulness that my husband made the bed and ensured I had some coffee when I got up. The more I thought about it, the more things I found to be grateful for.

It's a lot harder to come down on yourself when you look at your day through a lens colored by gratitude. Sometimes, if I really think about it, I know I am highly blessed to have the things I have. It's not just about "It could be worse." I know it could be worse, but I do not need to focus my thoughts on things that do not affect me at this time. What I have is right now, and right now, I can power walk a mile and a half.

FEED YOUR FISH

Emotions can be easily associated with water. Sometimes, it flows gently and you will feel at peace, seemingly with no effort at all. Other times, you are caught up in riotous rapids where your only hope is to cling to some small craft that has already capsized. Of course, there is everything else in between these two extremes. This is life, after all. There will be times when it just flows, and not much is going on, and other times, unexpected tragedy will leave you feeling as if you are drowning.

Life does not need your help in becoming more difficult, and if you are not living mindfully, you could find yourself "feeding the wrong fish." It is up to you whether or not you feed the koi of your emotional pond or toss meat to the piranhas. Like that old story of the two wolves where the old man warns his son (or daughter), there is a "good" wolf and a "bad" wolf fighting within each of us. The young person then asks, "But how do I make sure the best wolf wins?" The wise one answers with this: "The one that grows the strongest will be whatever one you feed the most."

With that said, I do not want you to beat yourself up about how you handled things in the past. Or yesterday. Or even five minutes ago. Wisdom comes with experience and practice. That old man in our wolf story probably knows exactly why one wolf became stronger than the other. He might have fed the wrong one for a good portion of his life as a young man. It was not until he began feeding the one he wanted to be the most like that his own life became a cautionary tale of wisdom for others.

Going back to our water analogy, we can learn not only how to effectively use the gentle streams of our lives to help us survive the rapids of despair and tragedy, but we can also create additional streams where we can rest our weary hearts and minds to recover, regroup, and tame the rapids. At the very least, give ourselves the skills and tools to navigate them without falling out of the boat of our thoughts.

HUNGRY HUNGRY PIRANHAS

Piranhas bring to mind something voracious that can take down even a large animal in a matter of minutes (Layton, 2008). And just like negative thoughts, one or two won't have much of an impact, though they can still take a chunk out of you. Physically or emotionally, depending on whether or not we are talking about the actual fish or an analogy for anxiety. The problem comes when you start entertaining these *piranhic* thoughts and allowing them to grow.

One negative thought easily leads to another. A natural concern about your husband being late and hoping they are okay when you've not heard from them for over an hour is easily dismissed once they've either returned home or grumbling about a traffic jam. However, if they're only five minutes late and you begin envisioning them being in an accident, you may find your thoughts boiling over as anxiety systematically tears through your serenity to the bone. This type of thinking can be tough to overcome until they arrive home safe and sound.

By then, you may be overly sensitive and snapping at little things because of the heightened emotion you have been experiencing. Just like that narrow miss from an accident you managed to avoid last week, your heart is still racing. It takes time to calm down, even after the danger has passed. Even an imagined one.

Anxiety is a hungry emotion, and it'll generate more anxiety if you do not get it under control. Of course, prevention is the best medicine, and that medicine, when it comes to overcoming anxiety and living a life you love, is living a life of gratitude. It is because of this that we want to strive towards this mindset. This is not something that happens right away, and you may have to begin this new way of thinking during one of your toughest moments.

If you find yourself caught up in a feeding frenzy when it comes to anxious thoughts, work to feed the other fish in your emotional pond. I like to use koi as an example because I've often seen them swim together in languid groups; their orange and white scales glinting in the sunlight. There is just something quite serene about watching them. Still, even they get hungry and will happily leap to any food you drop into the water for them.

Just as different fish will eat other things, piranhas tend to swim towards meat and koi towards rice and corn (San Diego Zoo Wildlife Alliance, 2020); different emotions can be fed and maintained based on the thoughts you are entertaining. The best way to starve anxiety piranhas is to instead provide the grateful koi some more palatable food for thought.

TENDING YOUR TANK

Perhaps you find it odd that I use analogies like fish and even wolves, but it's simply how I look at a lot of things. Some find it endearing. For me, it's just who I am. Speaking of "That's just who I am," I want to caution you from using that as an excuse to continue behavior that hurts either yourself, others, or both.

Usually, these types of things are not just a personality trait of who you are. Often, they stem from trauma and a desire to stay safe. You may not have learned how to deal with emotions healthily. Emotions are a part of life and are natural. Sometimes, it is necessary to express even a negative emotion, but it's important to do so in a healthy manner, be it anxiety, anger, or even sadness.

It's when it begins to not only interfere with your life but to cause those around you to make it a part of their own internal lives. Excessive anxiety in anyone can be very traumatic for yourself and anyone else around you. And because I do like analogies, we can use a tank full of fish to represent your emotions and the people in your life.

If you've ever had a fish tank, you know you must work to clean it every now and then. I remember growing up with a 10-gallon tank with colorful guppies. Guppies are very prolific if you have both male and female ones. There are many ways you can run your tank, but one thing is clear; a dirty tank is not very pretty to look at.

Sometimes, like with a fish tank full of guppies, you have to clean out the gunk in your emotional life. Occasionally, you might notice your fish are struggling and you do not know what is wrong or how to help them. To bring your fish back to health, or save the remaining ones, you might need to seek advice from someone already familiar with the problem. For this, you might make a trip to an aquarium or pet store where someone on staff could answer your questions and give you tips and suggestions on the best course of action.

If you struggle with constant anxiety and it's affected you to the point of not being able to function, then you too might need someone familiar with anxiety to help you. Keep in mind, I'm not a doctor or therapist. If your needs exceed the scope of this book, please seek professional help.

I do know what it is like to live with debilitating anxiety and if I can help even one person that reads this book, I will be quite satisfied. Hopefully, it helps more than one person. In the meantime, know that you are not alone. You are not helpless. Anxiety does not have to rule you. And if you take time to take care of your emotional health in the way that works best for you, you can only benefit from it.

2

SHAME ON YOU, FEAR!

Natasha (name changed to protect privacy) had a problem. For as long as she could recall, she was afraid of the dark. This led her to have trouble falling asleep unless a light was on and the closet door was shut. Nothing made her feel safe, even when she was later married to a wonderful man, whom she is still with to this day.

As an adult, being afraid of the dark ate at her self-confidence and embarrassed her. Even with her husband being loving and supportive, just the knowledge he had made her feel small and even outright stupid. Stupid was something she called herself frequently.

She did seek help many times over the years and was prescribed many different sleep medications and even several sleep studies. Sleep apnea was ruled out, and the most they could find was she had an extremely restless leg syndrome. It was suggested she had chronic anxiety, but this diagnosis left her feeling more ashamed than relieved.

Most told her to simply "snap out of it," but try as she might, she was unable to stop being afraid at night. Her feeling that everyone thought she was stupid caused her to see it in everyone's eyes and hear it in every tone. She began "mind-reading" everyone's ideas about her, which often left her alienating those closest to her. Most of all, it frustrated her husband, and a rift formed between them.

Natasha has never been sure what triggered her fear of the dark, though one could easily speculate. Speculation over what may or may not be the reason did not help her overcome it, however. As the years passed, the lack of quality sleep started stealing her health as well. Again, she sought doctor after doctor for help. Once more, anxiety was suggested, and it seemed completely crazy, at least to her, that anxiety could be a source of her sleep issues.

Jump to 2022 and Natasha not only sleeps better, but she is also no longer afraid of the dark. Even on a recent 10-day trip where she traveled and slept alone, she felt little anxiety. She missed her husband and family, of course. However, it was nothing she could not deal with, and she found the trip both refreshing and vitalizing.

So, what had changed? Natasha decided to take a look at her life and weed away the things that made her feel like a failure. She made some tough choices, but at the end of the day, when she checked something off on her "to-do" list, it consistently left her feeling as if she could never do enough or be good enough at it, and she would drop it even if it was feasible.

Some of her choices were dramatic. She wound up changing careers to one that fit her better. This was one of her biggest struggles, she discovered. Every time she worked outside the home, she would fall to pieces. And every time, she would claw her way back to a better place, feel better, and then go back to work. It took multiple instances for her to understand that working outside the home was not for her.

This did not mean she felt the need to be a "housewife."

Instead, she looked back at all the times she desperately turned to sales and being her own boss. She made a note of the times she felt content with where she was at. In the end, she decided to "work her business," as some called it.

It was scary, relying on herself and her own work ethic without the safety net of having someone else run the show. Yet, despite that supposed insecurity, she never felt more alive or more fulfilled when she established personal relationships with those she served.

And yes, that is how she views her career. One of serving others. And that was her true breakthrough.

You see, Natasha had a sister who, from early childhood, had both emotional and educational challenges. She loved her sister and witnessed her being torn down until her story echoed hers. Both sisters struggled with self-esteem, and it was this that triggered a desire within Natasha to find ways to help the women in her life understand they had worth.

All those other jobs, which she did excel at, had not fulfilled this desire to help lift other women. And while she understands how she and her sister are intricately tied together in their journey of self-worth, she has decided it's more important to move forward instead of dwelling on the past. She has determined to lay down the shame that was not hers, to begin with.

YOU ARE NOT WEAK BECAUSE YOU NEED HELP

Natasha's story may leave you wanting to know more, but for her, it was hanging onto a past she had no control over that led her to her anxiety in the first place. Her difficulty in overcoming it was feeling ashamed and weak in needing help. You may think there is no difference between what can be a root cause for chronic anxiety and what keeps you trapped within it, but you would be incorrect.

Many times, anxiety could be the result of something out of your control. In fact, it is this lack of control that may lead some to avoid seeking help. Seeking help may feel like losing even more control as you would not be solving your own problem. That problem is anxiety.

It may be of interest to you that choosing to seek help, be it from family members, support groups, or a professional with a doctorate, actually gives you more control. Not only does it take strength to admit you need a helping hand, but it can also give you the accountability needed to get started and stay started as well as the knowledge you are taking steps to improve the quality of your life. This knowledge can be uplifting and comforting and help you feel more in control in a positive way.

If that is not enough for you to look for help when anxiety has taken away your freedom to live your life in a manner that brings you contentment and even joy, then perhaps seeking help to improve your relationship with others might prove to be the motivation you need. This may prove to be a strange and self-defeating reason for seeking help and making positive changes in your life because we are regularly told we should not change for anybody. But is this really a bad thing?

KNOWING THE DIFFERENCE

There is this pervasive belief that changing for anyone you care about is foolish and should be avoided. We are often told that if they really love us, truly love us, then they will love us for who we are. I am not saying this is untrue. There are times we must be reminded that we are already good enough. By that, I mean that person at your core, when unfettered and refined (or at least striving for that refinement), should not be suppressed.

Let me give you an example. A young woman I have known all her life was vibrant, full of energy and smiles. She was a bit quirky and unafraid to share that with the world. In fact, if a song came on that she enjoyed, it was not unusual for her to stick her head out the window of my car and just belt it out to everyone around us. This, while stopped at a light.

In writing, this might sound awfully embarrassing, and I am not going to lie; it was a tiny bit embarrassing but in a good way. Her absolute joy in life was infectious, and it showed in her face and voice. It was as if a light within her shone brightly without fear. Because of this, it was difficult to remain abashed in the presence of such unfettered joy.

Then, there came a time when her light began to dim. No longer did she belt out songs in a silly voice. Her very being seemed weighed down. Suppressed. I began to wonder where the vibrant joy within her had gotten to. She had changed, and it was not for the better.

To make a long story short, she was in a relationship that took her time to get free of. Unfortunately, while with this man, he regularly gave her a hard time for her joking and lighthearted nature. There was more, of course, but let's leave it to the fact it was a toxic relationship, and that relationship had her changing who she was. More accurately, it suppressed who she was.

Though she did find the strength to leave this person, it required her to lean on others. It still took time for her to recover from this relationship. Even then, I was saddened by the thought she might be forever damaged from this, and her unique light might never shine quite as it had in the past.

And just like a toxic relationship can dim even the brightest of lights, so can a healthy one with a person who respects and loves you. It can bring you back to looking at life more positively. It can change you. In the case of this young lady, she met and married the love of her life, and suddenly, it was like she found her true self again.

I bring up her story to highlight that changing for someone can range from a horrid occurrence to a beautiful recovery. It's very dependent on who it is you are changing yourself for. If that person loves you and any habit or personality trait you have that is not toxic or hurtful to you and others, then they should not be pressured to change those.

However, if you are moody, angry, fearful, or have turned to things like drug abuse in order to cope, it can, and will, interfere with your ability to have healthy interactions regularly. If someone cares for you, they are naturally going to want these challenges addressed. They are going to want you to change.

Hopefully, their reason for encouraging you to make changes will be based on love and respect as well as concern for your well-being. With that said, it can be difficult to live with someone who has these behaviors. It would be normal if part of their reason is for their own relief and happiness. And they are allowed to want that.

SHAME IS AN ILLUSION

Now that we have covered some of the reasoning behind why you might or might not want to make changes in your life because of someone you love, I want to continue to tie in one of the biggest reasons people will not make a change even when it is the best thing for them. Fear. "Wait! Why are we talking about fear if this section of the book is titled "Shame Is an Illusion?" I will tell you why.

Shame itself can stem from fear, which is frequently tied to the anxiety response because of how fear and anxiety can trigger one another (Baton Rouge Behavioral Hospital, 2021). Shame covers up your fear and anxiety and is one way for you to avoid facing it, so you are not left feeling vulnerable. Simply put, it's a shield.

And like any shield, it is there to prevent damage. Unlike its physical counterpart designed to protect someone from bodily harm, the shield of shame is but an illusion. And an illusion cannot truly protect you. If you want to truly shield yourself, you must first find ways to deal with your fear and anxiety.

That does not mean anyone should treat shame as unimportant and dismiss it. While shame provides an illusionary shield that can help a person avoid dealing with fear and anxiety, it is a very real emotion and can interfere with healthy communication. Steven Stosny (2014), Ph.D, writes an enticing article about the dynamics of the shame-fear connection that assures the reader that healthy communication can lead to positive connections between couples that help alleviate both fear and shame.

START WHERE YOU ARE

I've brought up an online article where you can seek out insight for a reason. For many, seeking help and direction, as mentioned earlier in this chapter, might be difficult due to feeling both shame as well as a foreboding sense of having no control over your own life. This can be greatly alleviated by seeking help online, in books, or in a way that protects your identity and makes you feel safe.

I want to be clear that this does not mean it would not be more appropriate for you to seek in-person or even group therapy. You, in the end, will have to take the steps and actions that will help you the most. Remember how I told you that when you take such steps, you are not giving away your control to anyone else? You are taking it for yourself. You are taking responsibility for your life and your self-care.

If that first step towards self-control starts with looking up online articles and reading books like this, then, by all means, start where you can! I've done both types of research and attended therapy both individually and in a group. Sometimes, that group includes only my family or very close friends.

It's important to keep in mind you can start anywhere in your journey toward being anxiety free. By that, I mean chronic and debilitating anxiety, of course. If you are most comfortable starting with online resources, start there. If instead, you prefer to talk to a professional, I encourage you to do just that. In my opinion, getting started, even in the smallest of ways, is better than not getting started at all. Just start somewhere.

If that leads you to need a personalized plan and even medication, there is no reason for you to feel embarrassed or ashamed. I understand you very well might feel exactly that. I know I did. However, just as I became determined to gain control of my anxiety and, therefore, my life, I want to encourage you to do the same. Again, just start where you can and go from there. It sounds so cliché, but I'll repeat it. One... step... at... a... time.

There are other ways you can begin gaining more control and confidence in your life besides looking things up online, reading books, and seeing a specialist. Just take a look at your phone. You can browse many helpful apps that include ways to overcome your anxiety. I will cover these and other resources you can use to help you remove toxicity and fear from your life, as well as how to maintain freedom from it or the occasional life occurrence that can sometimes cause turmoil in anyone's life.

But, before we can move on, we must starve our anxiety. And that, my dear reader, is what we'll be covering next. So, let's get on with it and reclaim our strength together.

3

STARVING YOUR ANXIETY

Not everyone escapes anxiety or fear. They may wallow in it for decades. Some never recover from some of life's harder hits. It's easy to look at them and think, "If I were them, I'd do... " You might be able to successfully put yourself "in their shoes." You might even be very good at doing this, but instead of doing that, I suggest taking a moment and simply feeling compassion.

The reason I am prefacing this next story about an anxiety survivor and not immediately getting into it at the start of this chapter is that it's incredibly difficult to write and could be triggering to some. If you have experienced abuse as a child and need to skip to the subsection after it, do not hesitate to do so. Additionally, this book is not aimed at helping children or young people through abuse or the resulting anxiety (or any other consequences).

It does, however, aim to try and help adults. And some of those adults have suffered significant trauma leading to extreme anxiety and fear. Again, I warn you that the following content may be triggering.

WARNING! TRIGGER CONTENT: A VICIOUS CYCLE

Lynne is an older woman in her 60s. She carries herself hunched over as if she could somehow protect herself from the world around her. She cares deeply and has a heart of wanting to help and never be a burden. To all those she does not live with, she is that sweet lady that everyone immediately feels endeared.

It is not the same for those that live with her. Decades of passive-aggressive behavior and alcoholism made it easy for those close to her to wonder why anyone else would put up with her. Her daughter, who cares for her these days, was frequently asked such questions over many years.

While this story is not necessarily the story of the daughter of Lynne, she and her younger sister have been traumatized because of their mother's fear and the deep pain she suffered as a young woman. It is only by the grace of God, according to her eldest daughter, that she has been able to look at her mother and see her through the layers of prickly behavior and spiteful words during drunken bouts and other brief but painful episodes.

Anxiety can be a family issue. It can begin from early child abuse from decades ago that feeds into that now-grown child's fears causing them to turn to self-medication that frequently leads to their behavior becoming similar to the one that previously abused them in ways that scar their own children. Instead of searching out ways to heal, they hide behind layers of pain so deeply rooted it seems an impossibility to make changes as far as everyone else is concerned.

But change at any age is possible. Lynne's pain from her childhood abuse was multi-layered. Her story only came out in bits and pieces over the decades. Many of which she only spoke of while deep into a bottle of blush wine, or worse, vodka. Like finding a thread in an intricate tapestry, Lynne's eldest daughter was able to see the bigger picture and understand her mother a bit better.

There were so many times the daughter, whose name is purposely being left out if you have not noticed, felt at her wit's end. Her own pain and anxiety from growing up with someone who had never recovered in any way from extreme trauma led her to need time apart more than once throughout her lifetime. Many would think she was an idiot for allowing her mother to come to stay with her this final time. Especially after what had happened that caused her mother to be forcibly removed from their home more than five years ago.

It started out as a pretty good day. It was a Friday evening, and the best friends of the eldest daughter and her husband had been invited over. There had not been a serious episode with her mother, so she had not paid much attention to what her mother was drinking. Not until she was so drunk she began a rant telling her daughter's best friend how "she killed my grandchild!" while they were sitting on the front porch that day. Not only did this completely shock both the daughter and her best friend, but it also caused a stabbing emotional pain within her.

The accusation was based on how the eldest daughter and her husband had lost their first baby at 14 weeks gestation. For some reason, her body was not expelling the now-deceased unborn child, and to her horror, her obstetrician, or OB for short, told her she needed to get a dilation and curettage (D&C) procedure. It's a very similar procedure to when someone gets an abortion.

At the time she and her husband had given Lynne this news all those years ago, Lynne was drunk. The young couple had been staying with Lynne to save money for their little family, and unknown to them, Lynne had walked down the road to where her own father lived. He, too, was drunk.

This, of course, was not unusual, but on her return home, Lynne kicked them both out. She had become convinced her daughter and son-in-law had decided to get an abortion. It did not matter how many times they tried to explain what was really going on. So, on top of losing their baby, they were now homeless. At the time, they had no idea it was Lynne's father that had fed her this belief during his own drunken state at the time.

This was many years ago, by the time the rant occurred on the front porch. Lynne was completely enraged and abusive in the treatment of her eldest daughter, which prompted her daughter to grab both her boys, who were teenagers at the time, and order an Uber to take them to a nearby bowling alley where both her husband and her mother-in-law were participating in a Friday night league.

The reason the daughter ordered an Uber, though she had a car, was because she realized she was way too upset to drive. Upon arrival at the bowling alley that evening, her mother-in-law saw how distraught she was and immediately consoled her and the boys. Her husband, however, was a bit quiet and said very little. When they had finished bowling, he immediately took his wife and boys home.

They say it's the quiet ones you must watch for, and in some ways, this is quite true. Once home, the husband witnessed first-hand a full-blown drunken rage of his mother-in-law. He attempted to calm her down initially, but as bitter filth fell from her mouth about how horrible her own daughter was, he became very angry on behalf of his wife.

Despite being very angry, he remained mostly calm. However, since, in his view, she could not see reason nor calm down, he called the police. By the time the police arrived, Lynne had progressed to screaming obscenities about her daughter and even began offering blow jobs to both her son-in-law and the male police officer.

As you can imagine, this did not help the situation at all, and her son-in-law began to ask the police to remove her from the home so she could "sleep it off" in jail. Yet, despite all that had been said about her, Lynne's eldest daughter begged both the police and her husband "if we can convince her to go to bed in her room" to allow her to be free and in the morning, the husband could drop her off at her sister's house, who had already agreed to take in Lynne after being appraised of the situation.

You might be tempted to think this is merely a story about a drunk woman saying and doing terrible and stupid things, but what it really should highlight is that this was all a reaction to trauma, sexual abuse, and the loss of her husband in a shooting accident that left her with two very young daughters she could no longer emotionally connect with. Her pain was simply too deep at the time.

A compassionate person might see Lynne as a person suffering greatly and not a drunken monster. Smart people will tell you to cut such people out of your life. However, a wise person may see both the behavior and the reason behind it and take steps to provide support and an environment that encourages healing. They also know when to take back and regroup their energy to be able to refill an emptying reservoir that allows them to maintain their calm.

Lynne's response to trauma long ago did not display itself as an alcoholic; she was also agoraphobic, a condition that makes a person afraid to leave home due to intense fear and anxiety she had never faced. Her anxiety and fear prevented her from creating healthy relationships as well as preventing her from recognizing the blessings she did have.

This realization of the blessings she had received whilst living with her eldest came crashing down on her the morning she woke from her drunken rage the day before. She was sent to live with her youngest daughter and son-in-law. Unlike her eldest daughter, who had sought help to better handle her own anxiety, and so on, the younger sister had not.

This resulted in Lynne living in the home of a hoarder with no transportation between any of them. This was a blessing in disguise as it meant Lynne no longer had easy access to alcohol due to them not living anywhere near a store she could walk to. This forced sobriety over nearly two years was not welcomed at first, and she blamed her eldest daughter for "ruining her life."

But she could no longer hide her misery in a bottle. During this time, she began interacting with a group of people online. These were good people, and they lifted her up and encouraged her to make changes. These changes wrought such a difference within Lynne that one day she picked up the phone and called her eldest.

There were tearful apologies that eventually led to lengthy conversations between the two of them. Lynne begged to return as she could not stand living in filth due to the compulsive hoarding of her youngest daughter. It did not happen right away, but eventually, her eldest and son-in-law relented with conditions of "no drinking" and "Please respect my wife, and we will respect you." The fear this would only be temporary was strong within the eldest's heart, but now that she knew her husband was fully behind her and would ensure her mother complied, they brought Lynne back into their home.

It's been five or six years since Lynne has been living with her eldest daughter. She still attends the online group that first helped her see there were things she needed to work on. Since then, she has also participated in other groups that helped lift her up. While she still grapples with a lot of suppressed memories and pain, she has slowly worked on overcoming her tendency to hide behind alcohol and passive-aggressive behaviors.

She has been accomplishing this not only because she continues to surround herself with positive people, but she has also applied their suggestions to replace the more negative habits with something else she finds far more enjoyable. For her, this is mostly her Bible and history study and working on the family tree.

It does not take much thought to see where her interests lie! She loves history wherever she finds it. At night, when the house-

22

hold sits around the table, it's not unusual for her to share some lost tidbit in the family history or some other interesting find while pursuing the internet. The way her face animates and her eyes twinkle, it's hard to believe that this now elderly woman had spent decades suffocating in fear and anxiety.

A FAMINE FIT FOR ANXIETY

So, how did our dear Lynne bring some measure of peace to her life? You could say it was her new online friends. Well, not so new these days as they have continued to be uplifting friends for years. In many ways, you would be correct that these changes were because of such uplifting friends. However, it was not just that.

While Lynne was spending time engaging in a positive activity among people who cared about both her and the family she lived with, she was not feeding her anxiety or fear. What started as Lynne using them as a sounding board to complain about her eldest daughter while feeling stuck living with her youngest became gentle accountability where they encouraged her to work on her own behavior. "You cannot change someone until they are willing to change," they reminded her.

Because of this loving reminder and encouragement to work on what she could change, which was herself, she began to see how she was responsible for many of the conflicts that had come between her and her eldest. She began to take some responsibility, one tiny step at a time. It was these steps that led to her reuniting with her daughter. And from the daughter's point of view, she felt as if she finally had a mother she could talk to. They even shared interests and conversations that were healthy and fun.

Such deep seeded anxiety and fear cannot be quickly erased, and life continues, along with the normal ups and downs. There have been some blowbacks, but because their mother-daughter relationship is built on much sounder ground, it's a lot easier for them to work together to a resolution both can live with. And the way they accomplish this is simply by working to put their focus on something good. When you do something that lifts you up with another person, it tends to elevate that relationship in many ways.

Anxiety cannot live on a diet of positive social encounters, and making time to do the things you love and seeing the people you care most about is one of the surest ways to reduce it. Every moment you spend doing something where the focus is on something that encourages growth and healing is another moment you suck the power from both anxiety and fear, which will eventually starve it into submission. Just as these negative emotions tend to feed on themselves, so does consciously taking positive actions that build uplifting experiences. In essence, you are rebuilding your courage by providing it with the things that fulfill you while starving fear and anxiety.

YOUR EMOTIONAL MEAL PLAN

Just as you can eat food that endangers your physical well-being or prevents you from being in prime condition, so can consuming an unhealthy emotional diet. If you have long-time habits that need to be changed, whether it be the food you eat or the way you deal with painful things, if you want to be the best version of yourself that you can be, you need to do what it takes to achieve that.

For the body, you might choose a new meal plan and exercise regime. But how do you do the same to change from an anxious life to one full of vibrancy and hope? They say, "You are what you eat!" and the same can be said about how you think and feel. You are what you take in.

If you take in fearful news headlines, endlessly scrolling through warnings of war and our society falling apart, you are teaching yourself to think in those terms. However, if you instead fill your time with happy moments and interactions regularly, this will become who you are given enough time. So, the next time you find yourself spending more than a few minutes catching up on the news, it can be good to stay abreast of what is going on in the world today, make a conscious effort to seek out something that reminds you there are also still good things and good people to learn about.

This is not merely about doing things that distract you from any anxiety you may be feeling at any given moment, though sometimes that is exactly what you need at the time. Instead, you must work on actively making the necessary choices to do the things that help you live a life you love. It will be up to you to discover what it is you love and grow your appreciation of it.

Be careful about only consuming an emotional diet of things to do that never involve other people. Conversely, it can be very beneficial to spend time alone simply enjoying a beloved activity. It isn't that you must balance the two. There really is no such thing as a perfectly balanced social/family life with those periods you need to retract from the world and spend time alone. At least not in a general sense.

For some, they need more positive social time. I stress "positive" for obvious emotional and mental reasons. Others are more seclusive and need to spend more time in their own company. And so long as they enjoy their own company, they can continue their personal growth on multiple levels.

The key is that these experiences are being used to cultivate a fuller and more enriching life. You will always need at least a little bit of both. And some days, the amounts required could be vastly different. You cannot always be a "loner," and neither can you always be a "social butterfly." But, some will be more drawn to one over the other, and there is nothing wrong with that if the reason behind it is a healthy one.

DON'T STARVE YOUR BODY, STARVE YOUR ANXIETY

Eating well can have a tremendous effect on the way you feel, both physically and emotionally. One of the ways you can help starve anxiety and fear is to simply feed your body in healthier ways. Perhaps you do need to make better choices when it comes to the food you eat, but you do not need to attempt to create and follow a strict meal plan or spend money on one that is made for you. Instead, you want to be intentional and aware of the food you put into your body as well as your emotional and mental state.

If you are unsure whether or not you are eating a certain way due to anxiety or fear, there are ways to determine this. According to a list found in the article "How to stop stress eating for good" by Grace Jauwena (2019), posted on the Life + Health Network, there are simple ways to tell the difference. The article lists for us one of the most obvious signs, at least for me, that highlights how quickly hunger overtakes you. If your hunger is a sudden and acute desire versus one that slowly increases over time, chances are it is a hunger based on stress (Jauwena, 2019).

It can be surmised that anxiety can be stress-inducing, so being aware of something like this can help you find control in an area previously neglected. Once you understand you may be stress-eating because of anxiety, you can take action and turn it into something positive. Even the simple act of drinking a glass of water when stress-induced hunger assaults you can help you regain control long enough to seek out an activity that calms and refreshes you instead of shoveling food into your mouth mindlessly.

Even if you do, I want you to know that I, too, face similar challenges and do not always handle them perfectly. It's all too easy to beat yourself up about the times you fail rather than remember all the other things you accomplished that very same day. Each day you wake up is a new day for you to take another step or make adjustments that will help you do exactly that. And each action you take is one you can have control over, even if only in the smallest of ways.

Control is an important aspect of turning anxiety from something that left you feeling helpless to someone that knows that not only are you accountable for your own recovery, but you are capable of accomplishing it. Making conscious choices of building friendships that lift you up, cutting out toxic habits like doomsurfing, where you keep scrolling through and reading bad news, or doomscrolling, which is doomsurfing on your cell phone (Merriam-Webster, n.d.-g) and being aware of what you put into your body can give you a considerable amount of comfort and control over your emotional well-being.

You might not be the one responsible for how fear and anxiety took root in your life, but you can and should take control and become the captain of your own life. In essence, you are the boss. So, fire whatever/whoever from your life that has become a constant source of all that is holding you back from a life you love living.

4

REPEAT OFFENDERS

W orry is a natural reaction when you do not hear from someone for days or even weeks when they usually keep in touch daily. Concern for the well-being of a loved one who has been in an accident is also quite natural. It is when these genuine concerns lead you to a gnawing fear that something terrible will happen each and every time your spouse drives home from work that it causes your body to react as if it has actually happened.

Imagine this feeling being experienced every day where your thoughts can vividly picture your spouse dying on the way home from work. Your thoughts go so far as to imagine the police coming to your door, a surge of despair fills your body, and you cannot relax or let go of that feeling until either your husband responds to your text messages, calls, or, better yet, arrives home safe. You are like the dog greeting its owner because, as far as it's concerned, you have disappeared forever (Andrews, 2017).

This is exactly how Jennifer (not her real name) felt. She knew it was silly to worry so much, but she still could not seem to control this anxious waiting once the clock hit a certain hour. For her, each minute passing felt like an eternity. Logically, she knew the chances of her husband not making it home were low because he was an excellent driver who had shown exceptional capability in avoiding dangerous incidents on the road.

This fear would even pursue her while in a car when anyone else but her was driving. This would put a strain on her interactions with her husband as he felt she did not trust his driving. She assured him it wasn't his driving she was worried about. It was everyone else's. On the surface, this seemed true. In truth, it was not a lie either.

Now, if you go back to when Jennifer was a young woman flush with the love of another man seven years her senior, you might start to understand how this fear of others' driving had begun to take hold. This man had been in seven accidents by the time he was 18 years old and continued to show a complete lack of defensive driving despite having to pay a very high premium on his insurance and taking multiple classes meant to instill within him a safer mindset when it came to safely navigating the road.

He was not merely an aggressive driver. If he had the right of way and saw someone else taking it when they should not have, he would take the right of way, even knowing, without a doubt, it was going to result in an accident. This made the previously fearless Jennifer terrified of allowing anyone else to drive her around, and this showed not only in her fears of her husband experiencing a roadside death years later that never happened but while operating as a passenger in other people's cars. It did not help that some drivers really are careless.

COMMON SOURCES OF ANXIETY

Jennifer's story highlights one source of anxiety that is quite common: lack of trust. Fear and anxiety are insidious maladies that can eat away the confidence you have in others' capabilities. Rebuilding your ability to have faith in another after having that trust broken can be very difficult. For some, it is a seeming impossibility.

It makes sense that Jennifer would become fearful of other drivers due to her previous relationship with a man whose driving had proven time and time again to be a danger to himself and anyone else on the road. During the course of their relationship, he was in even more accidents. It did not matter how she cautioned him to drive more defensively and that knowingly forcing the right of way in a situation that would cause an accident legally made you the one at fault in the state they lived in.

These additional accidents led to a singular disaster that had a serious impact on his life. One day, while driving the company truck he used for transportation to complete any active work orders, he wrecked the vehicle while crossing an intersection on the way to an assigned job. As insurance companies are wont to do, they did their usual investigations and quickly found he was at fault.

The accident had occurred directly outside a military base, so there were multiple reliable witnesses to what happened, including at least one guard stationed at that entrance. Not only did he become responsible for paying off the costs of the accidents, but he lost his job and his driver's license. As a result of his persistent lack of driving defensively, he was forced to move out of state and live with his mother.

This experience of Jennifer being in regular contact with someone who drove so poorly that it put her and others in constant danger of an accident led to her constantly thinking about it. This habit of mentally going over something repeatedly is referred to as rumination, which is rooted in the word ruminate, whose meaning refers to a more casual manner of thinking about something (Merriam-Webster, n.d.-h). Casual was not something Jennifer felt regarding her anxiety when it came to being in the passenger seat of any driver, regardless of whether or not they drove defensively and had a good record.

Of course, the capability of others to drive safely or not is not the only way a person can find themselves struggling with anxiety. Some of them might not have to do with anything that has happened in the past of a sufferer. Multiple medical causes have been linked to anxiety, some of which can have a genetic component (Mayo Clinic, 2018). However, just because you might have a disposition that can lead to anxiety more easily than someone else does not mean you have no recourse.

It's important to seek help sooner rather than later. The sooner you take action when you realize you are struggling with such mental turmoil, the better. It will be a lot easier to overcome endlessly repeating thoughts that cause you mental and emotional difficulties if you do so.

THE DANGERS OF RUMINATION

You might find it obvious, due to Jennifer's story, some of the dangers found in destructive rumination. For the most part, her experience highlights how it can cause roadblocks between people who care about one another, such as the rift between Alison and her husband when her fears lead to him feeling as if Jennifer did not trust him. However, there are other repercussions of rumination that can become increasingly detrimental the longer this continues. Because of this, I want to ensure you have a full understanding of this particular mental activity and cover just how disruptive this can be in your life or the life of someone you care about.

Rumination can prolong already-existing depression, anxiety, or even anger. It can also interfere with the development of healthy modes of thinking as well as processing emotion in a manner that helps you heal and grow. This can easily lead a person caught up in this dangerous cycle to feel isolated because they will push people away in an effort to protect themselves. They might even do this in an attempt to protect the ones closest to them.

Because a person caught up in this insidious cycle is effectively not thinking clearly, it can be difficult to understand what it is they are going through in their internal lives. This inability to easily connect with others who can relate to them ensures the victim of self-destructive ruminations feels even more isolated than before. For those of you reading, you may know exactly what this feels like from the point of view of the one sucked into a negative rumination cycle.

There are other traps when it comes to rumination. Perhaps you started off by mulling over a problem in an attempt to find a better understanding of an ongoing problem or situation. On the surface, this seems like a way to problem solve, and when handled in certain ways, it really can be helpful. But, only when it comes to your own actions and the portions you have control over. If you are so caught up in what you may or may not do instead of actually doing any of it, you will not have accomplished anything useful.

Another reason you might find yourself ruminating over something is when you have suffered trauma at the hands of another. Sadly, it is a vain hope that you will gain insight into another person's thoughts and feelings about why they did what they did. Even worse, you may replay certain scenes in your head over and over, trying to find ways you could have handled things differently so that there was a different outcome. This type of thinking locks you in the past. It seals you off from taking action today over the things you have control over.

Sometimes, we find ourselves in situations we really cannot control. This may lead you to continually think about the situation in a similar way you would think about a past event that has already come and gone. In either instance, you are better off focusing your thinking on something you do have control over. In the following section, we will cover some of the ways rumination can be used to improve your mental and emotional life to help you progress in a direction you are more likely to find contentment.

NOT ALL REPETITIVE THOUGHTS ARE UNHEALTHY

Remember when I covered trying to problem-solve using rumination? While this can easily lead to an unhealthy pattern of thinking, there are ways to utilize this tendency you may have as a tool that will be helpful in moving you forward out of a situation you are not content in. However, this transforms repetitive thinking into something called reflection.

Reflection is very similar to the act of rumination. Some describe rumination as "brooding" and reflection as "pondering" (Hwang, 2022). So, what exactly is the difference between these two modes of thinking besides having a different term applied to them? Brooding tends to focus all your attention on any problems you have as well as any potential outcomes. You are not truly problem-solving. Instead, you are mostly focused on yourself and everything that could go wrong.

When it comes to actively working on yourself and understanding your current position and any responsibility you carry when it comes to problems you face, reflecting on them will help you come up with workable solutions. It is when you take steps to implement these possible solutions that you've turned ineffective ruminating into a useful reflection that brought you to actively make changes using the insight you gained during the moments you spent pondering the issue at hand.

The biggest difference between brooding and reflection comes in where you focus your thoughts the most. Are you constantly thinking about what went wrong and beating yourself up about it? You are likely ruminating, AKA brooding. If, instead, you are working to understand yourself better and how you truly feel about a particular situation and taking the time to find a workable solution you can implant rather than bemoaning, "Why me?!" you are probably practicing the art of reflection.

As you can see, it is better to ponder over a situation rather than brood over it. When you use this effectively, you are less likely to avoid facing something you have the power to do something about. If you make an effort to cope with difficult feelings and situations, it becomes easier and easier over time to face them. Just as brooding over all the bad things in your life can make you feel more and more depressed, thinking about all the ways you can overcome those same problems can make you feel very empowered.

5

HAVE YOU HEARD?

Some things can scar the psyche even when you either have no memory of it, or it's shoved so deeply you cannot access it easily. There are also those times when you might not have had the cognitive understanding of what truly happened, and this can lead to a shadowy realm that can easily distort the view of those who lived through such an experience.

This lack of understanding can stem from a variety of reasons. Age can easily determine how you view and understand any given experience and how it is stored, if at all, in your memory. Drugs and alcohol can also alter your perception and understanding of an event. Sometimes, physical trauma can cause the mind and its ability to retain an accurate memory of what happened to fail completely.

You may be wondering if there is another story to be shared about an anxious person working to overcome a life full of fretting and worry, and there is. But it's not a different person than the one already mentioned. We are going to go back to Natasha's story. This was our friend whose fear of the dark left her traumatized on a nightly basis. Perhaps you had wondered what had led to such a fear. She certainly did.

Unless you have suffered through the trauma of waking nightmares, which were times Natasha woke up still caught in the throes of terror where she swore she could feel and sometimes see that which assaulted her in her dreams, you may be tempted to dismiss it as "no big deal." For Natasha, though, it was utterly terrifying. Her dreams were filled with horror and death. Strangely, there was little blood despite the extent of injuries friends and family suffered in these dreams. Often, the assailant was already gone by the time she stumbled onto these scenes as she dreamed of an invisible power that threatened her with bodily harm as well.

She felt helpless and immensely afraid while also grappling with what she considered an embarrassing fear of turning out the lights before bed. Even the security of having her husband beside her meant little once he was asleep. Perhaps it was because he was such a sound sleeper and her terror so great he never awoke to her soundless screaming.

Officially, such occurrences are referred to as "hypnopompic hallucinations" and are found in approximately 12% of people, and despite their potential for alarming the sleeper, they are generally considered normal (Summer, 2021). However, when it disrupts your entire life and leaves you exhausted on a daily basis, there is cause for concern. It is because of this concern Natasha sought out the help of her childhood psychologist.

People don't become a certain way from within some imaginary bubble. Natasha certainly did not wake up one day and go, "I think I'll have nightmares!" She felt suffocated by her fear and desperate to overcome it. Even then, her first time back in the office of her old family therapist had her wringing her hands, nervous and ready to be told she was crazy and needed to be put away. Additionally, she did not want to be medicated. She had seen friends and family that had become more listless and showed little interest in the people and life around them. Alison wanted to live, not escape.

Thankfully, she learned that this particular therapist worked with his patients using something called cognitive behavioral therapy (CBT). And if you recognize the acronym and are concerned, don't be. It has little to do with alternative lifestyles, should you happen to have been exposed to that. If you haven't, forgive me for bringing it up. I just know not everyone thinks of talk therapy when they see this particular combination of letters.

CBT

So, what exactly is CBT? According to Merriam-Webster (n.d.-b), CBT is the most studied behavioral science technique used today that helps people learn how to not only identify self-degrading thoughts but work to replace them with healthier patterns of thinking. It's proven to be quite effective in helping many people seeking relief from chronic anxiety and other mental health disorders.

You do not need to be suffering from any mental disorder to benefit from this technique. Everyone, at some point, will deal with stressful situations, and being able to better manage how you handle them can be both useful and provide relief in an otherwise difficult period. It can also assist you in coping with chronic physical symptoms.

The need to become more self-aware of your patterns of thinking, if you pursue this type of therapy, may be the initial focus of your first few sessions. Or however long it takes. There is no correct length of time, and each person works within the framework of what helps them overcome destructive patterns of thinking.

For Natasha, each session began with a simple relaxation exercise. She found a comfortable position, using pillows as necessary, and her therapist talked her through the relaxation of her entire body. He always started with the toes and slowly had her squeeze each muscle group and then relax them. By the time she got to her neck, shoulders, and head, Natasha discovered she held a lot of tension in her body on a regular basis.

This effort to help Natasha release the tension within her body is not one always described in the various steps a therapist will use during a CBT session, but a relaxed body tends to lead to a more relaxed and calm mind. According to Dr. Elizabeth Scott (2022), relaxing the body can break up and even counter a negative-feed-back cycle.

Because stress and anxiety can cause tension within the body, actively working on relaxing can pave the way toward a successful CBT session. Once the patient achieves a more relaxed state, the therapist can begin guiding them through any worrisome and even traumatic experiences they may have faced in the past or are currently dealing with.

Sometimes, the therapist may encourage a patient to make a mental list or call out any thoughts and ideas that come to mind that are unproductive. If needed, they can help gently tease them out until the patient becomes more comfortable dealing with them without prompting. Once an unhealthy line of thinking is identified, the therapist will help the patient come up with more positive and helpful thoughts to replace the formally disagreeable mode of thinking.

The therapist's goal is to assist the patient in learning how to relax, process, and replace unproductive and damaging thought processes on their own without the need for frequent sessions over time. Since CBT is typically considered a fairly quick way of making positive changes in a person's life, its non-invasive nature is appealing to many. It also works quite well in a combination of other therapies if deemed necessary, such as alongside a medication regime or when there is deeply rooted guilt, whether warranted or not. This brings us to a more recent type of therapy called acceptance and commitment therapy (ACT).

ACT

While ACT is not the only other therapy put there besides CBT, it has been building quite a lot of momentum within both the scientific community and among those who struggle with anxiety. ACT is frequently combined with yet another therapy with the acronym MBCT (which stands for mindfulness-based cognitive therapy). I know this might be confusing, so hang in there with me. We'll get through this, and you will see how beneficial both these are.

Acceptance and commitment theory is exactly what it sounds like. You accept something, usually, something you previously were not facing and felt a lot of guilt over, and you commit to facing that something. The goal, of course, is that you deal with the issue and emotions involved in a healthy manner rather than continuing to avoid them.

To accept something, you must be made aware of it, and that is why ACT is frequently combined with MBCT. MBCT uses meditation as a method to gain insight to help those who suffer from chronic anxiety, depression, and even chronic pain. Once you have gained the necessary insight into the thing, or things, that have been preventing you from achieving a level of contentment in your life that is beneficial, you must commit to taking the necessary steps to overcome these thoughts and feelings. This can help you take control of your actions and unchecked emotional backlash that has been based on whatever it was you were struggling with and/or guilt you had over any particular situation, and so on.

Of course, a lot of that might seem like a bunch of gobbledygook without some perspective, so let us use Natasha as an example of how she might use ACT. As we learned in Chapter 2, Natasha was ashamed and embarrassed by her fear of the dark.

Even the knowledge she had from the particularly gruesome nightmares that would explain why she might wake up terrified, desperate for light, did not alleviate the feeling of shame she had. She felt like a child who never grew up afraid of the monster under her bed or in her closet.

Natasha benefited from her CBT sessions with her therapist. It helped her relax and feel safe while discussing her overactions and anxiety when it came to her assumptions about how others viewed her fears. It was changing her behavior in these instances, but she found she was never good with making lists of her problems and then listing alternatives. She kept coming back to the same problem, which was the shame and the guilt she felt when reacting to the misread expressions of those she loved the most, such as her husband. ACT was not stopping her from "mind reading."

Because Natasha was struggling with accepting and dealing with her shame, it made fully applying the benefits of ACT difficult, if not impossible. While she found it helpful to attend sessions to get things off her chest, it was only a band-aid in her particular circumstances as she still had yet to face her true fear. The nightmares were merely a manifestation of what she feared the most. Not monsters or demons. Not unseen violent forces that threatened to kill or maim those she loved. It was a fear of abandonment.

Meditation had always been suggested to Natasha to help center and calm her, but every time she tried to sit there and relax, she just felt so antsy! Her body felt an undeniable need to just move. This actually made her feel even worse, and it was not until she started doing a daily stretch routine where she could slowly hold various positions for a brief amount of time before going to the next she discovered one did not need to sit still in order to meditate.

Just like those runners wearing T-shirts stating, "Running is my meditation!" not everyone reaches a balanced state where their mind and body finally work together as one, unfettered by what has been and what might be. They are in the moment, and that moment feels like endless potential. It is there, in this quiet vastness, that many can observe their feelings, experiences, and even trauma instead of reliving it.

Being able to be in the role of an observer can go a long way in helping anyone begin the acceptance process. For Natasha, the healing began when she realized she had a suppressed memory of her father's death. He had been accidentally shot in the heart, and there was very little blood despite the deadly wound. And she had witnessed it. Not only that, but during the shock of the event, no one had been able to stop her from going to him as he lay there on the living room floor of their small trailer.

Natasha had been quite young, less than two years old. However, even all these years later, she had the vague impression of trying to wake him up. She would not have understood, at the time, what force had stolen her father from her, and these impressions left a scar deep within her that expressed itself through her dreams.

The years following her father's death were not easy ones. It had torn her mother apart and greatly affected her ability to focus on what still remained. As a result, Natasha did not just lose her father; she was emotionally abandoned by her mother. As understandable as this might be to anyone who has suffered the loss of someone they considered to be their soulmate. It created an atmosphere where Natasha was made to feel she had not truly suffered a loss. After all, he was not her husband.

It was this knowledge of why she felt and reacted the way she did that led Natasha to be able to utilize the tools she had been given in therapy and begin to accept not only had she experienced a traumatic event; she had lost someone very important to her at the time. Her daddy was gone, and it was okay to have missed him. It was also okay to feel the loneliness she felt due to her mother's inability to accept the loss of her husband, Natasha's father.

Because of her meditation and finding the capability to face what had happened, she was able to accept that she had been a broken person. It also taught her she did not have to keep moving through life broken. She could take it and move on. She could begin the healing process and focus on the things she was grateful for.

ACT is not just about discovering what it is you've been having difficulty facing. Not everyone has a suppressed childhood memory. Death and other traumatic experiences can happen at any time in one's life.

As such, anyone who has experienced difficult times may use avoidance to try and make it "go away." And no matter how we might wish otherwise, ignoring a problem often does not solve it. It can even make it worse by creating additional roadblocks that lead to still more avoidance measures. Additionally, once these things are ignored for an extended period, it can become a deeply instilled habit that can be just as traumatic, if not more so, to over-come than the original episode that caused the avoidance behavior in the first place.

Acceptance can be a difficult step in the healing process, but it is a must if you are to overcome the things that have been holding you back. Once you have come to terms with your struggle and guilt and have accepted not only how it affected you but how you might have affected others around you because of your lack of acceptance, you can take the opportunity, as Natasha did, to commit yourself to move on.

CBT OR ACT? IS ONE BETTER THAN THE OTHER?

As you read over these accounts, you may wonder if one type of therapy is better than another. There is only one reason why one might be better than another, and that is whatever one works best for you. We are each different, with a different combination of experiences and challenges. It would be impossible for one to always fit all circumstances. So, whether you use CBT, ACT, or some combination of both, what really matters is what makes you capable of living a life of gratefulness.

And if you are wondering, "Why gratefulness?" that answer is both easy and complex. This might sound like a cop-out, but I've learned that knowing what works and actually doing it is easier said than done. You will need to remind yourself of these things or you will fall right back into the very habits you were trying to overcome in the first place. So, yes. Gratefulness is a key component in finding and maintaining a life that brings you contentment.

6

YOU HAVE MY GRATITUDE

I t's true. As the title of Chapter 6 says, you really do have my gratitude. I am thankful for this opportunity to not only share my own story but to learn from the experiences of others and refocus my own journey. Lord knows, I certainly do tend to fall back into old habits and ways of thinking that hinder my life in so many ways.

It's more than that, though. Since you've made it this far, I know that if you continue reading, you will be able to unlock within yourself the knowledge that you really can have a more fulfilling life. You have the power and capability to take control and no longer be someone that is always just reacting to the things that happen in your life.

Instead, by the time you finish this book, you will be well-equipped with tools that will help you step forward and take action on the things you thought you could only wish for. Wishes are passive, but doing something about them? That's power. So, let's take you from feeling out of control and wishful thinking into a life you are powerfully grateful to be living.

What exactly is gratitude? According to Merriam-Webster's

(n.d.-f) online dictionary, gratitude is "the state of being grateful." So, what exactly does it mean to be grateful? It's a common phrase to say things like "be grateful for the little things," but are little things the same for each person? One's "little things" can be another's wishful thinking. Which is precisely the point for remembering that though something is common in your life and easily obtained, it is not always the case in the lives of others.

While looking around for more ways that I could build more gratitude in my life, I came across an article written by Paulina Cal y Mayor Galindo. There was a lot that resonated with me in that "What is gratitude? 5 ways to be thankful" article. There was one quote Cal y Mayor Galindo (2021) used by Melody Beattie I found especially eye-opening: "Gratitude turns what we have into enough, and more. It turns denial into acceptance, chaos into order, confusion into clarity." Beattie continues these thoughts by saying, "it makes sense of our past, brings peace for today, and creates a vision for tomorrow" Cal y Mayor Galindo (2021). I usually like to rephrase things in a way I would normally voice them, but I found her words more than enough to convey what I was trying to explain.

Going back to the article that Paulina wrote that brought to my attention the words of Melody Beattie, there was one thing I simply did not resonate with. Well, I liked the general gist of what she was getting at, but her usage of focusing on the intentions of others when they give you a gift or do something nice for you (Cal y Mayor Galindo, 2021) feels like a slippery slope for those of us that live with an anxious mindset. We tend to "mind read" the intentions of another. Maybe I'm just paranoid. Oh wait, I have an anxious personality and have a bad tendency to believe that people's intentions and what they think about me are bad rather than good.

Does this mean her suggestion has no value for those of us that grapple with anxious thoughts and feelings? No! If we can use this mindfully and even ensure that we are strict with ourselves about this process, it can become a useful tool. Instead of defaulting to the thinking they must have some agenda, or they simply felt obligated to do anything nice for us—after all, we don't want their pity do we?—we can purposely steer our thinking in a more positive direction. I recommend just being grateful in that moment and not trying to mind-read their intentions.

HOW TO BUILD GRATITUDE INTO A LIFESTYLE

Some days, all I have is that little reminder my phone pushes at me. It tells me to take 10 minutes of my daily time to be grateful. Wow! Have you ever actually sat down for 10 minutes and written out things that you are thankful for? Or, perhaps you go into prayer. Either way, as that timer ticks by and you empty your brain of the things you are grateful for, such as a roof over your head, food on the table, being in a decent relationship, or just having the ability to read a book, the things you bring to mind you are grateful for are quickly exhausted, and you still have seven minutes to go.

Don't get me wrong, there are times when I can surpass that 10 minutes, but what do you do to take full advantage of that 10 minutes and realize you cannot get in even 5 minutes? This is when I play songs I know heighten my appreciation of what I have. For some, it will be worship music. For others, it will be a motivational speech or song. I've used both of those methods in the past and continue to do so to this day. It's a way to help you become more mindful and to help you stay in a frame of mind open to being grateful as well as motivated.

But gratefulness should not be delegated to a mere 10 minutes a day. While it's helpful to schedule these daily moments, you want to learn how to be aware of them throughout your day. It requires you to pay attention throughout your day to what others around you are saying and doing. If you are in the habit of noticing someone's negative patterns or the things you dislike about them, dedicate yourself to finding one thing that you admire in that person. Trust me; there is going to be something good you can find about any person. You just may not have seen it because you have been burying it under a mountain of annoyance or outright anger over some other thing or things you dislike about them.

This is not to say you should allow a toxic person to gain any power over you should this be the case, but if you are stuck with them, finding one thing you admire can make the difference between breaking down under them or staying afloat to get enough breathing room that you can take a fresh perspective, unburdened by your expectations. You might actually discover you've been contributing to the toxicity between you and another.

You cannot control another person, but you can influence them by taking control of yourself. And actively looking out for things to be grateful for allows you to focus on something other than what normally might lead to you losing control of your emotions, and so on. And once you start broadcasting the inevitable calm that comes along with not constantly focusing on the negative things, it will have a ripple effect. Others will respond accordingly.

You might have noticed this echoes some of what you have already read in this book because of the personal stories shared as well as the commentary about them. That is because, at the core of every success, a grain of gratitude is cultivated. It's tough to fight anxiety if all you see is what's going wrong all the time. Instead of being reactionary to everything around you, water that tiny seed within you whenever you can.

Gratitude is like the thirsty tomato plant, as any gardener may have discovered. For it to truly thrive, you have to take care of it daily. Ensure the soil is not drying out and keep it watered. You can also overwater it, and while some may disagree, there is a way to overwater your seed of gratitude. Life is not simply about always being grateful. While it should be a regular part of it, there are other seeds you need to both plant and water in the garden of your life. One of these seeds will be fortitude.

Building your fortitude alongside gratitude is one of those situations where one supports the other and vice versa. Fortitude can be bolstered by intentionally living a life of gratitude. Appreciation, another way to think of gratitude, can be maintained by having the ability to be fortified against the occasional floods and droughts life can bring us.

Let's leave the garden analogy for now and look deeper into what building grit, or fortitude if you prefer, looks like in conjunction with gratitude. I like to check official definitions with resources such as Merriam-Webster, which thankfully has a full online dictionary these days. I also want to take a peek into the perspective of what others consider fortitude to be.

The aforementioned online dictionary, Merriam-Webster (n.d.-e), states that fortitude refers to a state of mind. One that allows you to deal with danger, pain, or hardship with bravery and determination. In other words, you have the courage to stand in the face of whatever it is you are dealing with so that you can find ways to overcome it.

It sounds like a good quality to build up within yourself, right? I don't think it would be a poor guess if I were to assume you would like to have such fortitude in your own life, both personally and professionally. It's something I regularly feel the need to work on too. But am I incorrect in making such an assumption? Am I doing that dreadful mind-reading?

I know what they say about the word "assume": It makes an ass out of you and me. Still, an educated guess can work out just fine. Additionally, the occasional use of a word that is usually considered crass can help get the point across nicely, as well. I do not want to mind-read my reader's thoughts as I could be making myself look very poor indeed. With that said, there are times when it is perfectly appropriate to draw a conclusion, and I believe this one to be helpful to the goal of this book. Many, myself included, could all use a little more fortitude these days.

FORTITUDE AND GRATITUDE GO HAND IN HAND

Gratitude and fortitude really do go hand in hand. Like that old peanut butter and jelly or even older horse and carriage combination. Sure, you can enjoy them separately—so long as that carriage has become self-powered—but there is just something about the combination of two different things that can transform the experience. Or, in this case, your life.

Intentional gratitude can help build up your ability to withstand both your internal turmoil and the things outside of yourself. It does not matter whether or not you have any control over those moments while going through difficult periods in your life. When you have taken the time to put in the effort needed to eke out whatever gratitude and appreciation you can find for what you have in life right now, instead of focusing on what you might have lost or what you do not yet have, it will instill within you the personal strength required to get you to the next step.

We will be covering this next step in the following chapter. The thing about steps is they can usually be used to go both up and down. So, consider these steps to be a stairwell you must travel back and forth at times as necessary. You will always need to place yourself back on the step of finding gratitude each day to fully utilize its positive effects. You will also have times when you must draw on your personal strength. Life simply is not linear, so like that peanut butter and jelly sandwich, do not be afraid to build and add whatever works for you. Only you can discover the best combinations that work for you, and some days it might require peanuts for a little crunch, and other days a bit of honey to sweeten things up.

HELP WITH ANXIETY

Is that analogy too weird for you? I do like my metaphors. Something my husband often teases me about and loves about me. Good thing, because I am chock full of them. Still, maybe you need it to be put another way. Actually, I do not think you need me to do that for you. I am confident you understood I was merely encouraging you to use these ideas and tools and build for yourself something that works best for you. I occasionally like to skip the jelly altogether and add bananas and marshmallow fluff.

It's things like the above analogy and silliness that help me stop focusing on the negative and pay more attention to the things I am grateful for. It's too easy to take things in your life for granted, and, sometimes, you need to come up with a little creative thinking to put them into perspective. I'm grateful for my sense of humor and imagination. It allows me to write and express myself in ways that people find interesting. Well, most people do anyway. Shh, anxious thoughts. Go away.

This brings me back to how grateful I am you have continued reading despite some of my more quirky sections. Or maybe it is the entire reason you've kept with me. Does this mean you should be grateful to me? I sure hope so. It's always nice to be appreciated, isn't it? I think it's time to move on.

WHY AIM FOR CONTENTMENT AND NOT HAPPINESS?

There are pitfalls when you fail to make an effort to find and create gratitude in your everyday life. Not only will your personal fortitude be based on a weaker foundation, but your ability to be happy with what you have right now also becomes compromised. In fact, focusing on happiness is a straw house in and of itself.

Often, we confuse what we think will make us happy with what will make us feel content. We are led to believe we can only find happiness when we accomplish that next goal, get that promotion, or complete our "to-do" list. It can indeed feel good and bolster your self-achievement whenever you accomplish what you set out to do, but if it becomes the bedrock on which we base our lives, happiness will always be that "next thing."

The very nature of living your life will mean there is always more to do, more to learn, more to gain, and more ways to be that best version of yourself. Worse, there is this insidious thinking that being content can stifle your growth in many ways. If you dare to be content with the money you make, how will you ever do what needs to be done to increase your income and position in the company you work for? But contentment is not about settling for something and giving up the possibility of something greater later down the road. It certainly is not something meant to stifle your personal growth in becoming someone you like and are proud of.

You absolutely can look at yourself today and either focus on the things you've yet to accomplish and consider yourself a failure or look at what you have right now, this moment. This is where gratitude is meant to fit in. That sweet spot between what you do have and what you can look forward to later down the line if things work out the way you hope them to. And yes, it is okay to look forward to things that have not yet happened.

Just don't tie yourself to them so strongly that if it does not work out, your world feels shattered. Sometimes, it's really not meant to be. Sometimes, even better, it opens the door to something that will just blow your mind. It sounds like the usual dribble, but do a little research on the stories of people suffering the loss of something or what felt like the crushing of their dreams. There are plenty of examples of how such experiences opened the door to something better if you look for them. So, never discount what you currently have.

To dig deeper into this topic of why contentment is superior to the pursuit of happiness, we are going to look at a few solid examples for this reasoning. I'd say one of the biggest reasons has already been brought up: the detriments behind placing your focus on the pursuit of happiness. Another reason we will cover in detail is our view on what will make us happy. We will finish this up with how to turn happiness into contentment in a lasting way.

Oh, the pursuit of happiness. It's not just a movie where the word happiness changes out the "i" for a "y." The film, *The pursuit of happyness* (Muccino, 2006), is based on the book of the same name written by Steve Conrad and can be very inspirational in helping people feel more motivated to work hard for their goals in the face of adversity. Which is precisely why it's not the pursuit that mattered. It was not even the goal. If you have not had the opportunity to watch this movie, starring actor Will Smith—a personal favorite of mine—I do recommend it. As you watch it, be mindful of how this single father handles adversity.

Personally, I am glad the story has changed the spelling of the word "happiness" because, in the end, this father was not really pursuing happiness. He was pursuing money. Yes, we need money to pay our bills, and some (if not most) of us, have to work very hard to put food on the table and make ends meet. If we cannot find a way to be content with what we have at any point in our lives, we may be unintentionally living a lifestyle we simply do not have the means to support at that point in time.

Being fully aware of your current circumstances and ensuring you live within those means can help you avoid many pitfalls, including overspending or taking on more than you are ready for. Do not fall for the "fake it until you make it" mentality. You'll only be faking your way right into debt, whether it be financial or emotional. And emotional debt is a thing.

This brings me to the point that you might not actually know what will bring you happiness. I think a better word to understand what will truly make you happy is to replace it with the word "joy." Not everyone agrees with this sentiment but bear with me on this. Ask yourself this: "When was the last time I felt full of joy?" When you examine these times, it was not the money you made or winning a trophy that lifted you up. It was the experience that you had that went along with a particular success or accomplishment.

I have been the recipient of unexpected financial windfalls here and there. While these did make me feel happy and even quite excited, it is always temporary. While I enjoy being able to pay my bills and even do something special with the money I receive from paychecks, sales, or those rare financial windfalls, it will never be enough on its own. I have to keep getting more as I am unlikely to receive a lump sum that will take care of all my needs and wants in one fell swoop. As a result, it is a constant pursuit that can easily feel like a never-ending treadmill toward more of the same. Constantly chasing after the next paycheck increase or other opportunities to add to my income has not brought me joy, much less any sense of contentment. Frankly, it's stressed me out before!

There is a lot of talk along the lines of "It's not where you wound up; it's how you got there." In essence, it's about the journey. Some sayings might have been around for what seems like forever, but there is a reason for that. If you fail to find some enjoyment in the actual pursuit of what you think is going to make you happy, you might find yourself oddly dissatisfied. Especially when you realize there is more to do if you are going to move forward and grow as a person.

And it is this active growth of improving yourself in multiple ways over the course of your lifetime that is going to help create that sense of contentment. Sometimes, the things that bring you the most enjoyment can hit you with surprising and unexpected intensity. I had this experience four years ago, in the spring of 2018.

I remember how I felt when I held my first granddaughter as a newborn in my arms. It was this intense joy and an unfamiliar sense of contentment that seeped deep into my heart. Four years later, that is still something I feel each and every time I have the opportunity to spend time with her or just look at the shared videos and pictures my eldest has provided me with. In fact, I now have two granddaughters. More would be welcomed, but I do not feel like I am missing out because I lack more. All I feel is absolute contentment.

How to turn the pursuit of happiness into contentment that persists has a lot to do with accepting and being grateful for what you have right now. Not what you used to have and not what you hope to have, though hope is never to be underrated in helping you achieve goals and lead a type of contentment that does not threaten to stagnate you.

What do I mean by stagnation? How is it different from accepting and finding contentment in the here and now in a manner that alleviates things like chronic anxiety and depression? Stagnation, as you probably already know, is all about no longer growing as a person. It's also closely tied to giving up. You cry to yourself, "Life is just too damn hard!"

Not gonna lie; life can be very hard. The things I've read and witnessed others have gone through break my heart. I also know what it's like to be beaten down in multiple ways. I always find myself in this weird spot where I have great compassion for anyone who has suffered while feeling relief and gratitude that my own experience was not nearly as bad as others' I personally know.

Honestly, I've never quite figured out the magic formula that creates a person who refuses to allow what bad things happened to them in the past, even when atrocious, to prevent them from growing and learning how to better handle their personal cross. Why does one sibling suffer through the same childhood and live a life of stagnation while the other pushes themselves to overcome their challenging circumstances?

The thought that things like generations of alcoholism passed from parent to child over and over will suddenly stop in the case of a single descendant, even as other family members, from a brother to a second cousin (continuing the cycle in their own lives) always astound me. When you research the likelihood of a child of an alcoholic parent becoming one themselves, it's hard not to be impressed by the individuals who throw off the mantle that stifles them and carve a new path for their own family.

And in case you are wondering, it is four times more likely that a person who grew up with an alcoholic parent will become one themselves at some point in their lives (Emily, 2021). If only that were the only negative impact for those who were raised in such a situation. We won't dig into those. However, if you are interested in more information regarding this subject, please check out Emily in the reference section at the end of this book.

I want to go back a couple of paragraphs to explain why I say cross instead of a word like "baggage." In my experience, the term "baggage" has this connotation that implies that the person carrying the weight of any type of trauma is somehow not worth the time to get to know or stick with them as a friend. Or more. Expressions like "Wow, she has a lot of baggage" are demeaning in my view. You might not have the fortitude to carry whatever cross another person bears, so let's not reduce their experience to mere "baggage" someone may or may not bring into any relationship.

Moving on. We know life can be difficult at times. It is not unusual to wish for a life where you get everything you need and want that allows you to never worry again. Sadly, this is not only going to become immensely boring, but it can also lead to the stagnation of character and spiritual growth. It does not matter if everyone agrees on the best type of growth, but development does need to occur if we are to achieve true contentment.

HOW TO FIND YOUR CONTENTMENT

Finding contentment goes hand in hand with finding your gratitude. There are many ways to accomplish this, and one of the most common is to simply make a list of the things you are grateful for.

Sounds easy, but for a great many, myself included, we need something a bit different. Because of this, I want to provide additional activities and resources you can explore that will help you not only learn how to be more grateful but recognize the things that make you feel content.

One thing that works best for me is listening to music that also highlights the things I am grateful for. You may even recall I do a similar thing when it comes to running or whenever I need a motivational boost. There is a reason that listening to music can help us feel more positive and energized. In fact, this phenomenon has been explored by psychologists as well as noted by anyone paying attention to how both themselves and others react to any given song or musical experience.

An example of this can be found on the Psychology Today website in an article by Shahram Heshmat (2019), Ph.D. The author has surmised that listening to music can lead to the release of dopamine, a chemical that occurs in a type of neurotransmitter found in the brain. This might explain why one can alter the way they feel and even relieve any stress that they are experiencing simply by playing their favorite song (Heshmat, 2019). Feeling good is not the only response you can experience from music, so avoid listening to anything that makes you sad or even angry. You want to add to your ability to cope with a given situation, not sink deeper into the mire.

Listening to music that lifts you up and making lists are only two of the ways that can help you generate gratitude that leads to contentment. If you find yourself dwelling on the past or excessively worrying about the future, take time to consider the here and now. Even taking 60 seconds to pause and breathe in a measured manner can help calm your thoughts enough that you can gently guide them in a more fruitful direction. After all, focusing on the things you suffered from in the past or engaging in wishful thinking is not going to help you find contentment.

I want to make it clear there is a difference between worrying about the future and making preparations in the event of a weather emergency or even building a budget that helps you to save for retirement years down the road. A little foresight now can greatly alleviate potential anxiety-inducing experiences where you feel helpless. You cannot prevent every possible outcome but you can take simple measures that will increase both your feeling of safety and a sense of calm.

In some respects, all of the above relate to your self-care, especially when you make a decision to do these things in an effort to improve your control over anxiety and fear. Still, basic self-care can easily fall to the wayside and can directly impact not only the way we feel about ourselves but add to our anxiety. If we do not take care of our bodies, such as regular exercise and eating well, there will come a time when we realize we are not happy with the way we look or how we present ourselves.

I'm not just talking about being overweight and smelling bad, though those things can certainly affect our self-confidence. Your level of fitness and hygiene, when overlooked, will suffer and are further proof of living a life of intentionality. But, there are even more consequences of not engaging in regular self-care. Your health can suffer.

If every time you look in the mirror, you do not like what you see, there are always small steps you can take that will lead you to a healthier lifestyle, more energy, and the confidence of knowing you are taking care of yourself. Feeling healthy simply feels better than being out of shape. Having the strength of the body can lead to the strengthening of the mind.

Taking showers and brushing your hair can have a surprisingly positive effect on your mood. I had an experience where I kept trying to meet up with a friend, and she would always cancel at the last minute. I eventually learned from her husband she had fallen into such deep despair she had not brushed her hair in a very long time. It was extremely matted, and she needed help overcoming this but was too embarrassed to ask for help from anyone outside of their home. And if you are asking yourself why her husband did not help, I admit I wondered the same thing, and this is one of those stories I will not delve into deeply other than to highlight this particular topic of self-care.

Regardless, I went over and, together with others in the household, we took turns helping get the massive snarls from her hair. Admittedly, I was initially convinced it would need to all be cut off and regrown, but patience and love have this way of making what seems impossible something you can accomplish. It did take a few days to completely overcome this challenge, but I was very proud of her for not giving up. By the time she could sweep her thick, heavy hair into a ponytail again, the effect was immediate. She felt so much better, and it showed in her body language and the smile on her face.

To say she was grateful for the help and the love behind it would be an understatement. It also made me thankful for the experience where I could help someone feel better. And this is how we will end this section—with a call to action. Find opportunities to help others, and not only will you experience their gratefulness, but you will also enjoy the experience. And who does not feel at least a little grateful for those times when you are the hero of another's day?

ANXIETY CANNOT FEED WHERE GRATEFULNESS FLOURISHES

I know these ideas and suggestions are already implied and even covered in other areas of this book, but knowing how to generate gratefulness on the fly is an excellent method for combating anxiety and even depression. We've spoken of taking care of your emotional garden. When you take the necessary actions, such as purposefully seeking out things to be grateful for, your garden will flourish and be a mentally safe place for you to retreat to whenever you need time to decompress.

When your emotional garden is well-tended on a regular basis, anxiety simply cannot entrench itself deeply into your life. As with weeds, it's always best to catch them early on in their growth. Neglecting to take the time to seek out opportunities to show gratitude to not only others but yourself can lead to roots that have sunk in deep. Pulling them will be painful. Still, even if you are just now beginning your journey of gratefulness, it is better to just pile it on top of the anxious thoughts and attitudes. Even weeds can be turned into compost that helps keep a garden fresh and lovely.

7

REMOVING TOXICITY FROM
YOUR LIFE

I am going to get really personal with you. I'm not even sure
how to word this other than bluntly. My marriage had been in
turmoil for 14 years. Yes, 14 years. The first several years were
quite good. But, if you recall from the introduction of this book,
my anxiety had reached heights that had a severe impact on my
own children. But it did not affect just them. It also affected the
communication between my husband and me, which of course, led
to problems in my marriage.

My husband's way of dealing with the tension between us was
to escape into gaming. His preference was massively multiplayer
online role-playing games (MMORPGs). He spent considerable
time working with others to help bring down *boss mobs* during what
is called a *raid*, where a large group of players used teamwork and
strategy to accomplish this. These raids would take up most of his
evenings after work. As far as I was concerned, he was married to
his computer. To say this upset me would be an understatement,
and it did not help me manage anxiety well. In fact, it made it
worse.

Even couples who start out strongly, even for years, can fall victim to habits and poor coping skills when difficulties arise. Latent general mistrust in others that had nothing to do with the other person may lie dormant until a challenge puts strain on the relationship. My anxiety had always been there, but for the most part, my husband was kind and loving and did not trigger my attacks into something that was difficult for me to handle. I was managing my long-term anxiety, but I was not actually facing it and developing coping skills that would help me weather the normal ups and downs of a marriage.

Enough time had passed, and I now know what triggered the change for the worse between us. The irony is that it did not start with something either of us did. We were both innocents of wrong-doing up until a certain point. To make a long story short, my husband was told something by a mutual friend we both trusted. However, what was said was an outright lie. And it was about me. This trusted friend led my husband to believe I had sexually propositioned him.

Can you guess what happens when two individuals, both with deeply hidden insecurities and barely controlling anxiety, are faced with an accusation like this? On my husband's part, he did not bring it up. He did not ask me about it. In fact, I had no clue that he had been told this lie. His own insecurities led him to believe it was true. He never felt like he was good enough for me by the time this lie made its insidious way between us.

Top it all with my own long-term anxiety, barely kept in check, and the recent birth of our youngest son, I fell into a deep depression. I've always been a bit of a go-getter, so I sought help from my long-time family psychologist. He then referred me to someone that could temporarily prescribe me something to help me get through it. That was his opinion, anyway. That I just needed a little help. Again, I did not know what was on my husband's mind.

I won't go into detail about the ravages such medications had on me. We learned over the years they tend to have the opposite intended effect and would make me worse no matter what combination we tried. I was hospitalized multiple times as a direct result of such medications adding to the overall stress. As both my husband and I declined into this pit that seemed determined to pull us further and further apart, he dug in even deeper into his chosen escape mechanism: gaming.

Because of this habit of his, I felt isolated from him. Like we were simply roommates living together. Somewhere along the line, I had come to the conclusion my husband needed to make changes. I was not wrong in thinking that if he made certain changes, it would improve our communication with one another to help our marriage. What I was wrong about was the belief he was the only one needing to make improvements. And like many other people, I was certain I could change him if I talked to him about it.

And talk I did. For hours. I do believe my feelings have merit, of course, and I desperately wanted him to know and understand where I was coming from and how much I loved him and wanted things better between us. I understood that communication is vastly important between any long-term couple, and I pushed and pushed for it.

Unfortunately, I gave him little room to express his side of the story. I was so busy trying to get him to understand me that I was unable to truly understand what was going on in his mind. I had so many assumptions and pretty much did the talking for him, which only increased his own feelings of inadequacy. He was full of insecurities he had never shared but was well aware of my own anxiety and worry that he did not know how to express his point of view in a manner that would not make things worse.

In retrospect, and after a lot of healing, I can appreciate my husband still trying not to make things worse and even still working to protect me, even with all the pain that was broiling between us. Still, his lack of confronting things, including the lie that had been forced between us by someone we had both trusted, only led to me becoming more and more anxious. My behavior became erratic, and I started seeking validation wherever I could to help me feel better about myself.

You might find it easy to lay all the blame at my husband's feet for believing someone who lied about me without even questioning it. They had given no proof and he did not seek any. He also never came to me with this false rumor or even confronted me about it. Not even in anger. He simply believed and treated me accordingly. Because of this, a large part of me would be hard-pressed not to agree that all the blame belonged to him, because if he had been able to talk to me about this terrible accusation, we could have avoided a lot of heartaches.

My own anxiety and insecurities had already been brought into the marriage and provided much of the stage that allowed this mistrust to grow between us. This mistrust was based on our personal insecurities that had been developed during our youth, making it easy for each of us to feel we did not really deserve the other. We were easy targets for someone with their own agenda, and gaming was an easy escape for him.

I had my own escapes, of course. Neither of us handled things well, and we were both at fault. Still, we both now share a strong angst for the person who told him such a devastating lie. But we also understood the lie would have never taken hold like it did if we had a healthy sense of self-esteem and been more trusting and able to share our inner selves with one another.

Communication takes at least two people. Otherwise, you are just talking about yourself without regard for what another is thinking and feeling. There is also the challenge of trying to mind-read the person you are talking to, which can lead them to shut down even more if your guess is incorrect. And yes, you are assuming that they have not been sharing with you to let you know what they think and feel and why they think and feel the way they do. You may fail to see that they, too, have challenges and insecurities. Finding ways to communicate with anyone requires you to take the time to listen. Do not just explain yourself and what you want to happen.

I know couples counseling works for many who struggle with communicating successfully in a marriage or any other relationship, but for us, it was a dead end. In retrospect, I realize most of the reason behind this failure was because I was more focused on what I thought my husband needed to change, such as spending less time gaming and more time with me, instead of seeing what pushed him towards that behavior. I was not "listening" to him.

It did not help that he wore a facade of "everything's fine" so well around others. Even professionals did not break through it. They did not even know it was there. As for me, I was convinced I was the problem in many ways due to my lack of knowledge of what triggered this mess in the first place.

Listening will not always have anything to do with what another says. Sometimes, it is what they do not say that can help you better understand them. My husband was "talking" to me by diving deeply into gaming. He was telling me something important if I would only pay attention instead of wallowing in my own feelings.

It never occurred to me to examine the effect my chronic anxiety had on him during those 14 long years. Simply put, as I later discovered, he had no clue what to do or how to help me through my intense anxiety. I later understood how helpless he felt. Gaming helped him escape his own sense of failure. His own anxiety!

Of course, something had to happen before I was able to unlock these truths from him. I had to stop worrying about what he needed to change and instead work on being the wife I wanted to be. Up until I decided to do just that, I was not that wife, and I hated it.

Does this sound old-fashioned or outright backward to you? It really shouldn't. While your opinion might differ on what makes a better wife or any other title, such as being a better parent, friend, and so on, the end result will be the same when you shift your focus from improving another to improving yourself. It was not about fitting some outdated idea of what being a wife is for me. It was a process where I worked to be someone I could respect and even admire.

My journey to having a better marriage started with me working on being the best version I could be of myself as a wife. It was not just about improving myself, though. Instead of trying to change my husband, I took the time to go out of my way to do nice things for him. It was nothing spectacular. Things like setting up the coffee pot for the morning or ensuring I switched out his towel in the bathroom for a fresh one.

These small acts of service not only made me feel better about myself as a person, but they also opened my eyes to the people around me. It taught me about how often these little things made others feel respected and cared for. And when I took the time and made an effort to treat my husband with more respect, I started to notice something quite interesting.

The people around me, including my husband, started doing the same thing. That is, he began making changes in his own inter-actions and responses to me. His constant gaming dropped dramatically, and we started to interact in more positive ways without me having to hound him about it. He, too, started doing small acts of service for me.

They say like attracts like, and it seems this can also apply to the way we live our lives. The people around us become far more likely to gravitate towards us not only when we start doing the things that bring us contentment in our private lives but when we find ways to serve one another, even in seemingly small ways. Strangely, this improvement in my marriage was not something I expected. When I began my journey of becoming a better wife, my only intention was to simply find peace with myself.

Even if you believe such a thing cannot possibly work, I recommend you give it a try. Try doing small acts of kindness and service for those in your household. Especially with those whom you have trouble with regularly. If you are anything like me, it will, at first, just be something you test out. I really did not have anything to lose at that point in my life, and neither do you right now.

I am sure you can tell there is a whole lot more to what was going on during that difficult time in our marriage. I understand your curiosity and possible disappointment. I am not going into all the details and will be skipping some altogether. One major factor that prevents me from delving deeper into that mess is the fact that it would take another book on its own to cover the trials, fights, and near destruction of my marriage. There were times I could not fathom how we managed to get through it. It had become outright toxic at times, and if I had not begun the work of discovering who I am and working on the things that brought me contentment, with or without my husband, I am certain we would not be married now.

But this book is not about the rise and fall of my early marriage and its near-miraculous recovery. It's about how anxiety and fear contributed to the circumstances that led to such dark places. And so I leave it to what is already shared so we can move on to how you can remove toxicity from your life that can, hopefully, help you escape what I had to learn the hard way.

YOU CAN HEAL A TOXIC RELATIONSHIP

Not all marriages or relationships discover healthy ways to improve communication in order to clear out persistent toxicity. For some, each day brings emotional turmoil and uncertainty. They will feel as if they have no recourse or escape. Many times, friends and family may not even realize what is going on. Many of us like to put on a "good face" so we do not look like failures, whether or not such a self-inflicted thought is true.

Every day, all too many adults will continually expose themselves to the emotional and even physical abuse of another. The classic example involves a woman and a man, where the woman is typically the victim. I am not here to berate or give excuses for why some people do not leave these situations. What I can say is this: There is usually a way to escape, though that does not mean it is easy.

As always, my heart goes out to those who never escape, and not once will I blame them for staying. Until you have been there for yourself, it can be difficult to understand why they stay. It could even be success stories similar to how my own marriage went from being extremely volatile some days and quiet misery other days to one that has a far more solid bedrock of mutual and self-respect for one another that keeps a person tied to someone that was never going to make healthy and positive changes. Honestly, it can be very difficult to tell the difference!

But what of the more complex situations where one person is a caretaker of an adult child that requires assistance, a spouse with a chronic condition, or an elderly parent? It can be emotionally and physically draining to care for someone, especially if that person was previously independent or struggles with the knowledge they are no longer able to take care of themselves without help. Not everyone wants to rely on the service of a family member, no matter how sweet and kind they are. Their pride might be pricked.

But this is no ordinary pride. It can be an incredibly difficult and humbling experience when you know someone else has to take care of you. Not only that, if this extends to even the most basic of care, such as bathing and toiletry assistance, it can lead to resentment not only in the heart of the one being cared for but for the person, or persons, that are caring for a person in need.

I am not discussing elder abuse or any other type of abuse, though that can certainly occur in extreme circumstances where the relationship breaks down over the intense stress involved in caring for another adult human being who can no longer do so for themselves. Anxiety and depression are common in both the caretaker and the one(s) under their care. If they are not addressed regularly, it will be impossible for the caretaker to give the best care they can as well as maintain their own well-being.

For the purpose of this book, I am focusing on what it is like to be the caretaker of a difficult or even outright mean individual. Unhealthy behavior, such as passive-aggressive outbursts (think of slamming doors and cabinets that are not merely an accident), a failure to respect the caregiver, and even sabotage can be frustrating and outright painful to deal with on multiple levels. This type of situation is actually covered, though glossed over in some ways, in a previous experience that was shared.

Remember back in Chapter 3, where we covered the story of Lynne and her eldest daughter? Lynne had spent a number of years living with her daughter, and her drinking was not only triggered by a difficult and abusive childhood. She also resented living in her daughter's house. She felt she had no say. No power. Yet, she knew she had very few, if any, options on her own.

It was not unusual for Lynne to walk through the kitchen of her daughter's home, slamming everything she touched. The cabinets, the forceful shoving of turning the faucet on, and the rough handling of her coffee cup would naturally lead those around her to ask, "Is something wrong?" to which she snarled a resounding "No!" Now, I do not like to try and mind-read people, and you do need to be cautious in doing so, but if you do not always slam stuff around as a matter of habit and only do so during times when upset or angry, people are going to question being told there is nothing wrong.

While Lynne was a difficult person to live with back then,

everyone in the household did want her to be happy. When she behaved in such a manner, it was not unusual for someone to try and solve the problem. Unfortunately, Lynne herself was the problem, as no one had done anything that warranted such an extreme response. Lynne could not stand being wrong, and even when the truth was in her face, she would steadfastly cling to her side of things. Even when it could be proven otherwise.

It was difficult for anyone caught up in this to respond in a manner that would diffuse the situation. The common response would initially be an annoyance that could grow into full-blown anger as those living with her would feel as if she was, personally, calling them a liar. This actually fed into her belief that she had no say or power over her own life.

We also learned how Lynne's behavior so disrupted her daughter's household that she was removed from her eldest daughter's home for a few years and stayed with her other daughter. After some necessary time apart, Lynne was no longer drinking and had made some limited progress when it came to dealing with all the pain she had been suppressing for most of her life. She still had a long way to go, but she sincerely regretted her words and actions that last day at her eldest daughter's home.

Lynne's eldest daughter had been prepared to cut her mother from her life completely because of the effect it had on her own emotional well-being. Because of this, she was quite reluctant to allow her mother to come and live with them again. However, after multiple heartfelt conversations over the phone, where mother and daughter faced some of their demons together, it eventually led both her daughter and Lynne's son-in-law to agree to allow her to return to their home.

Her relief at being allowed to return was apparent, and she was far more in control of herself than she had been previously. There was a light that had begun within her because of her involvement with a group that supported personal growth and recovery. Not only that, but it also helped stop her from using her daughter as a scapegoat for all her problems. This alone was enough to help pave the way to healthier interactions between the two of them.

It was not always easy to maintain peace as both women had strong personalities, even without the old toxicity between them. Over time, the relationship between these two adult women has become much healthier. They discovered a shared interest in their family tree as well as the drive for spiritual growth that strengthened their relationship even further. Because of this, they are regularly engaged in several activities together, including participating in group events with the same people that had to encourage Lynne to make positive changes.

I, for one, am so thankful for the many resources available to caregivers as well as those dealing with past experiences causing a disruption in the lives of those living together or looking to find ways to heal rifts between themselves and others. You can easily locate many of these resources online as well as in your local community. Resources found on websites such as health.gov and sometimes discounted WebMD can help reduce challenges similar to what Lynne and her eldest daughter suffered. They can even point you in the direction of seeking professional help.

It does not matter if you choose to avail yourself of the resources online, in person, or a combination of both. These organizations and private groups can provide much-needed resources that can simply make things better for all involved. Even better, you will likely find others nearby that understand exactly the challenges involved that will provide support in multiple ways. In some cases, they may advise that you separate yourself from someone whose toxicity affects you so strongly it causes your anxiety to skyrocket to the point you are now struggling to stay in control of yourself.

Not only will you find a lot of encouragement that helps anyone in the role of a caretaker or any other relationship that has become difficult or toxic, but they also strive to make sure you take the time to care for your own needs. It is very true that if you do not take care of yourself, you will find it more difficult to manage anyone else. So, do not neglect to refill not only your emotional tank but tend to the self-care necessary to help keep you capable and strong enough to continue this task that can all too often feel more like a burden rather than something that expresses your love for another human being in need.

WHEN YOU NEED TO CUT TIES

If you are in a caretaker's role for someone mentally ill or with a medical condition like Alzheimer's where the person is sometimes nasty, and so on, you may feel there is nothing you can do to help mitigate its effects. It may very well feel like a no-win situation. There are ways to put space between you and the other person if certain circumstances, such as a medical reason being the true source of challenge, require it.

You may need to make tough choices and/or find ways to take a break. Go on a local vacation and so on, even if it's only to spend the day at the beach or park, stay at a friend's house for a few days, or find someone to temporarily switch places with you so that you can go back to being a caretaker of a difficult person with a steady heart and unburdened mind. However, you are not obligated to be abused, no matter the circumstances.

Living in a toxic relationship, whether it be an older parent, a spouse, or just a friend, can be a continual source of fodder that kills you from the inside out. There may be times you must sever the relationship entirely. Especially if it puts you in danger physically, gaslights you into losing control, or becomes such unbearable that thoughts of suicide afflict you.

We've mostly covered ways to help heal a toxic relationship that either derives from severe anxiety or has led to the creation of fear that is interfering with your ability to engage in healthy ways. Sometimes, you can initiate positive change just by focusing on your own goals and self-improvement. However, like with the oft-spoken Lynne, there are times when the best thing to do is separate yourself from someone that has put you in a position where you've become reactive and easily gaslighted.

Gaslighting is a tool that the wielder can use to control another extremely well. Its effectiveness is usually based on the fact it's done slowly, bit by bit, over an extended period. Because it's initially a rare occasion, the victim can easily attribute it to the abuser having a bad day. Because everyone can have the occasional bad day, right?

Except, in the case of gaslighting, it's not just about handling a bad day poorly, which can happen to anyone if it's bad enough. The one gaslighting is working towards the victim becoming dependent on them by convincing the victim they cannot trust their own reality. This can cause them to question whether or not they recall events correctly or that others, according to the abuser, are lying to them. Leaving the gaslighter to become the only person the victim can trust.

Over time, the victim loses their self-confidence and might find themselves isolated from everyone but the person that has been gaslighting them. Gaslighting is not limited to romantic couples. They can occur between family members, friends, and even co-workers. If you are finding yourself questioning your own reality and ability to maintain emotional or mental capabilities to the point you are relying on a person who is also undermining your self-confidence, you should seek outside help as soon as possible.

Even if it really just is "all in your head," you should be reaching out for help. If the person making you question yourself to such a degree is not encouraging you to seek professional help lovingly, you would likely benefit from separating yourself from them until you do receive support. Once you are more sure of yourself, it will be easier for you to make decisions based on a reality you are confident of that does not keep you in a constant state of doubt and anxiety.

Not everyone will be able to successfully overcome a relationship where extensive gaslighting is involved. If your own anxiety or other problems have led you to become a gaslighter, know that you can make changes that will help you engage with others in a healthier manner. No one can "fix" you any more than they can "fix" anyone else. You can, however, work on yourself. Anyone can make a conscious choice to improve themselves, so it is up to you to make that happen. Once you have identified that you may very well have been a part of the problem, or even most of it, you have the power to change it.

One of the most difficult things a person can deal with is facing who you have been and what you have done. It takes strength of character some do not have. If it helps even a little, I want you to know this one thing; You are not weak if you admit to being wrong or doing wrong. Unless, of course, you are unwilling to do anything about it.

As tough as facing your own imperfections might be, it might be even more difficult facing those you have harmed along the way, even while trying to make up for what happened. Some people will not accept you no matter how much you have changed. As painful as this might be, you must move on. There will be others who will take you as you are now. The past is truly in the past, so long as you are not repeating such behavior as gaslighting to get your way again.

Before we close out this section, I am going to leave you with a few resources. You can also check the reference section for assistance should you need help. One important number you can call is the National Domestic Violence Hotline. They support many languages using interpretation services and have both English and Spanish speakers available 24/7. The number is 1-800-799-7233. If calling is either uncomfortable for you or not available in your area, you can always go online to their website at www.thehotline.org/.

Other resources for those who are suffering abuse as an adult by a parent can be found on hopefulpanda.com, livewell-withsharonmartin.com, and many others. Because some may be caretakers for difficult and perhaps outright abusive parents, you can look for such websites supported by www.alz.org, for the Alzheimer's Association, and www.seniorlifestyle.com. All these pages have multiple resources to help you as a caretaker should that be the need, and I urge you to use them as necessary without reservation.

8

MAINTAINING YOUR SANITY

E very day, Sarah wakes up to check her phone. She does not care what the news is going to say. What she cares about is utilizing a tool she discovered on her phone that helps her manage her expectations and her days. Sarah knows she could use paper or a special notebook, but she prefers the digital format. At first, this made her feel as if she was "doing it wrong," but after a while, she realized something: It worked for her.

Before, anxiety had her procrastinating, but she now has a plan. Part of that plan is the simple act of drinking water as soon as she gets out of bed. To make sure she does this, she places a water bottle by her bedside before going to bed.

Her water routine is part of an hour-long relaxation period she allows for herself. She finds making time for herself works well in setting herself up for success each day. The hour is hers to do with as she wishes, and, sometimes, she wishes to go ahead and tackle her first important goal for the day.

Sarah's next goal is her daily personal study. While she has set aside 30 minutes, this is not set in stone. She uses a study guide to keep her on track, and when she completes the lesson she has chosen, she moves on with her day.

It may seem like Sarah has nothing important to do if she can ease into her morning slowly, but giving herself a set time limit to relax gives her structure. This helps her utilize self-control more effectively. Without structure, she is easily distracted by things that add nothing to her day. If she is not mindful of her time, all her morning goals slide into her afternoon goals, and things can begin to crumble.

Not only does Sarah make time for her first two goals, but they also help her feel more ready to tackle her sales business as well as write her first fiction novel. Sarah lumps these two together because she has found if she leaves them separated, her mind takes it as "too much," but if she combines them, she has the freedom to prioritize one over the other based on the needs of that day.

To feel truly productive, she must spend some time working to meet her work goals. These goals, in turn, move her towards financial goals that are important to her. She usually only works Monday through Friday in her home, and this is the schedule that works best for her.

The rest of the day is rarely left to whim once she has completed her work goals. If she allowed this, she might find herself playing *Shop titans*, a role-playing shopkeeper simulation game, all afternoon with nothing to show for her time. So, she remains diligent in finding ways to loosely structure her afternoons and evenings, as well.

"Loosely" is the key for Sarah. She is far less likely to stick to a rigid, inflexible routine. Flexibility is not the only thing she must have. Every day, she makes time to find something to be grateful for. This has helped prevent her from freaking out when she cannot get everything she had planned for the day. Not only that, but because she is taking time to note the things she got to do and got to have, she often realizes she really did do a lot. This always makes her feel a lot better about her accomplishments that day.

Of course, there is more to Sarah's day than her morning routine and making time to be grateful for what she has. Sarah also takes time to take care of her body by exercising multiple days a week and eating well. It's not always easy, but she starts each day as if it's another chance to get another win.

Self-care involves more than exercising and eating well. Every day, she schedules time to pamper herself in small ways. One of the things she enjoys is taking time to do a skincare routine. It always leaves her skin feeling soft and beautiful. Sarah cannot pinpoint why this helps her. She just knows it does.

By the time Sarah has completed her exercise, the afternoon has arrived, and she eases into another work-related session that often never makes it past the two-hour mark because people start coming home from work, and her focus is interrupted. Dinner time is not far off, so she wraps things up and gets ready to spend time with the family at the dinner table.

Dinner is a time of sharing for her and her family. It's the one time everyone can catch up with one another while enjoying good food. Sarah is always grateful for this time and always looks forward to it. It can get rather rowdy, but that is part of the fun.

Even though Sarah is very much a social creature and enjoys spending extended time with those she cares about, she has found that making time doing something that she, alone, can enjoy has an amazing way of ending her evening on a positive note. After she has made an entry into her voice journal where she makes a note of the things she is grateful for as well as any thoughts she had while studying, Sarah likes to go relax with a good book. Lately, she's been setting aside 30 minutes to read a non-fiction book first to grow her knowledge and understanding.

After the 30 minutes are complete, she reads something just for fun until the edges of her wakefulness begin to blur, and her eyes start to drift closed. It is at this point she closes her reader and sets it on her window sill. Sleep may not always come quickly, but she is pleasantly nestled in a gentle weariness as her mind slowly shuts down the chatter of the day, and full sleep tugs her under.

MAKING PROMISES TO YOURSELF AND KEEPING THEM

It's easy to read about Sarah's routine and think "Wow, she has it easy!" She does not have it easy. Some weeks, she feels as if she is fighting a never-ending battle against anxiety, but every time she wakes up and sees that bottle of water she placed on her bedside table the night before, she remembers she has a plan. And for her, that plan is a promise she made herself broken down into manageable pieces. Each day is another day she can place those pieces throughout her day that brings her closer to her goals.

You see, being free of anxiety is not her goal. Anxiety is simply a symptom, as far as Sarah is concerned, that points out there is something in her life she has lost perspective on and she needs to make time to change that perspective sooner rather than later. It took time and careful examination, but she realized that anxiety rarely had a strong hold on her if she put gratefulness into her daily plan. It is that gratefulness that has helped her gain a more positive perspective on life.

I know we've been over a lot, and some of it had a bit of skimming over when it came to personal details about the stories we have covered, but the point was never for it to be an exciting reveal of other people's problems. They were meant to be tools to help anyone who reads this book overcome any anxiety that has taken over their life. Additionally, it shows the reader they are not the only one who suffers the backlash of things they may not have had any control over at some point in their lives.

In fact, you may have found yourself feeling like "Hey, that's my story!" and surprised that others have had all too similar experiences that left them feeling as if they were broken. I'm not going to pat you on the head and offer platitudes of how you are not broken, yet beautiful. You've probably heard all that before.

Maybe you are broken. Or at least feel that way. I know I've felt broken some days. Sometimes, much longer than days, if I am honest with you. But, as I made the decision to stop complaining about a life I was unhappy with, I started taking steps to do the things that brought me a sense of accomplishment and satisfaction, it made it easier to ferret out the things I am grateful for. I may not have lost all the weight I gained due to an illness, but I did make a promise to myself; I would take the steps necessary to help me return to my former glory.

I use the word "glory" because that is how I feel about it. I wish I could tell you that if you do a step-by-step process you will never ever feel inadequate again. That anxiety won't rear its ugly little head in your business. It is going to happen again, but if you promise yourself to look for the things you do get to have and experience, you can smash that ugly bugger to pieces. In other words, it is gratefulness that kills that particular beast.

A LIFE YOU LOVE LIVING

Think back to a day when you had this quiet peace of mind. If it's difficult to remember such a day, don't worry. You can create it for yourself. And not just one day but a week and even a month. Next year, you could be looking back with a smile, knowing you actively worked to keep the promises you made to yourself. That promise was to make time to be grateful each day. To dig out whatever small thing you could to remind yourself you are worth making an effort for.

So, what does it mean to live a life you love? Perhaps that is the wrong question. Let's try this one instead: What are the things you can do that help you feel as if you've had a good day? That still feels a bit too broad, but that's okay. At this point, I hope you've picked up one of the biggest things to practice throughout your day, which is gratefulness, of course.

So, you look at your life, and all you can think of being grateful for are things you consider unimportant. Things other people you know have. So, what if you have a roof over your head and food on the table? So does my next-door neighbor! I could admonish you by pointing out that this is an ungrateful mindset, but just by writing this sentence, I've done exactly that.

Still, I know what it is like to have a difficult time getting around your own internal woes. Sometimes, we have to try something new. Something to distract ourselves from that unhelpful and, yes, self-centered thinking. Get outside and look around you. I don't know if you are in the city, in a suburb, or surrounded by fields, but one thing should be made clear. You are rather small. This smallness may seem the opposite of what will help you, but if you can put things into a wider perspective, you might be able to see all the blessings around you. Breathe in and know you are alive.

Now that you are outside, walk to the end of your street or even just your driveway. Is the day clear, or does a storm loom nearby, and the wind is whipping your hair? Take it all in and allow your body to move for five minutes. Keep walking for five more minutes.

Next thing you know, you could have been walking for 20 or more minutes while you looked around you. Let's call it an exploration of the area you live in. When was the last time you truly experienced this small part of the world? As you return home, take one last breath and bring the expanse of your experience from outside into the house with you. Or apartment.

Wherever you live, you want to hold onto that feeling and make it a part of who you are and where you live. At this moment, this is when you ask yourself, "What am I grateful for?" You will likely find this an easier question to answer than before you took your little walk. I encourage you to do this daily. Put yourself outside, even if only for five minutes.

Walking outside is not the only way to start building a repertoire of things you can be grateful for. There are likely things you've told yourself over the years "I wish I could... " Only you can fill in the end of that sentence. One of my own personal wishes was to get back into singing in a choir. I love singing. Singing is an easy thing to do every day, yet I somehow managed to always put off practicing it.

When I decided I was going to just do it and I did, it took me a bit to find where I fit best. Previously, as a young woman, I was an alto, so naturally, I decided to practice alto parts. And it sucked! I could not hit those low notes like I used to. In my mind, I could not sing soprano either because, in my youth, I could not hit those very high notes. Which is why I was placed in the alto section. It wasn't until I was belting out songs just because I enjoyed them that it finally dawned on me I was now a soprano.

I share this with you because there may be things in the past we gave up on for a long time. Either because we just never got around to it or we had a limit. In my youth, I had always wished I could sing soprano, but I had the range of an alto. I did not care that, technically, it could be a harder part to sing, and being able to do so correctly was something to appreciate. In fact, I did not enjoy it until I lost the ability to sing well because of an illness that damaged my lungs in 2004.

To continue on, while it took a long time, I was able to sing much more easily, but I still stuck to alto. Never dreaming of trying soprano once I recovered. It was only when I was determined to get back into singing and join a choir did I learn I was not an alto. In fact, my fear of even trying soprano had me stepping back, thinking I needed more practice before I could sing with a choir during events. It was during one of that choir's events that it struck me that I was now a soprano. I could have face-slapped myself.

Still, I am grateful for the experience. It taught me something new about myself. It actually does not matter that I could not sing the alto part as I had thought I could and, therefore, had to step down to practice some more. What mattered is that I tried and discovered I could practice soprano parts from here on out. And that is exactly what I continue to do!

The goal here is to be living a life you love living, and this needs to be imprinted onto your mind. Whether you love fishing, camping, reading, playing games (both board and online), singing, or even knitting, it is making the time to do these things that will help build that life. It won't be the paychecks that pop into your bank account you will remember. It will be how you spend your day.

And if you are ending most of your days wishing it had gone a different way, you're doing it wrong. Still, on days like that, you can decide to look for the good parts and put your focus on them. Even if the best part of your day was eating French fries in your car, savor that moment and be grateful you got to have French fries and have a vehicle in the first place.

MAINTAINING GRATEFULNESS

We've already brought up gratefulness quite a bit by now. Hopefully, this repetition has impressed upon you that it's necessary to create a life you love. Living a life you love is not just about going for walks and pursuing hobbies you have neglected in the past. Or, perhaps had not even dared to try. It's about treating yourself and those around you with consideration.

There are habits you want to explore, grow, and perhaps even master that will add quality to your life. Unfortunately, there are also habits that you may have developed that will do the exact opposite. If you are to cultivate and maintain gratefulness that ensures you live a life you love, you will either need to steer clear of things like addiction to alcohol, drug use, cigarettes, and even using other things, such as gaming, to hide away from your feelings. None of these things will bring you lasting contentment. All of them, especially when abused, will hurt you and those around you.

So, spend time with friends and family and stay away from places and circumstances that make it more difficult for you to overcome habits that keep you from growing as a person. Take care of your body by eating well and being physically active. Be sure to get enough sleep and rest. Take care of your mind by sharing your thoughts in a place you consider safe to do so.

You will also need to learn how to set realistic goals. This book is not about goal setting, really, but I will leave some links in the reference section to help you get a handle on that. The sooner you focus on being the best version of yourself that you can be, the sooner anxiety will have to exit the floor of your mind. You have other awesome things taking their place because you have begun to develop new skills and do the things you love. Do not be afraid to challenge yourself by doing the things you thought you could not do. You are far more capable than you give yourself credit for.

If you feel like you cannot afford to try new things, I want to assure you that there are plenty of things you can do for little or no cost. Doing anything using your feet, such as walking, running, and even hiking, can easily be done at no cost. You might even find low-cost events such as a 5K that is welcoming to entrants of all levels. Or, you can use free apps on your phone or join virtual events. Do a little research, and you will find a bevy of support and ways to keep you going.

There is a site called Like Hack you can find online that provides a lot of tips and tricks on things you can do when bored.

Or just needing to find ways to flush your life out with something that brings it both meaning and enjoyment. You will find one of Life Hack's articles listed in the reference section for you to pursue at your leisure. It will cover 50 ideas that are low-cost that may surprise you (Johnson, 2015). If you need more ideas, ask the people around you. You might find them quite happy to help you find something you like that you can do together.

9

A NOTE TO LOVED ONES

I've seen movies, books, and articles both online and on the cover of magazines stating to anyone that cared to listen or read the things "such and such" wish you knew. You'll see something along the lines of "What men wished women knew" and "What your daughter wished you knew." If you want to get really specific, the movie *10 things I hate about you* (Junger, 1999) might resonate with many. Not just because it's a great movie but because it highlights that the poem written near the end of the film by Kat, the protagonist, played by the sassy Julia Stiles, was not about hate. It was about love.

And this is what I wanted to focus on in this section. Not just the things people with severe anxiety wished you knew about them, but that they need to be loved just as much as the next person. I sure hope that if you are reading this, it is out of love and a desire to help someone.

I can give a very personal perspective of what it is like from the inside amid a panic-induced reaction. It can come out as anger, fear, and, sometimes, even depression. My heartbeat will become very noticeable to me, which not only tells me my emotions are on the rise but can actually make it even harder to calm down. This is the worst possible time for someone else to become angry at me. I'll either shut down or go into a more aggressive mode. Fight or flight is the classic term, and it seems like the perfect description of what is happening to my body at that moment.

If you make even a short search on the internet about the chemicals being dumped into your brain during things such as a panic attack, you can quickly surmise it takes time to flush them from the body. One of the better articles on the internet that can be found is on ideas.ted.com, which is owned by TED Talks, where Ceri Perkins talks about the science behind panic attacks.

Perkins also covers what you can do to manage them. And while it is up to the sufferer of panic attacks and other debilitating moments to follow through on the things that will help prevent or reduce the intensity of future episodes, sometimes they just need help (Perkins, 2021). And you knowing both the science behind such things as well as what helps the best can turn a volatile relationship into one of a healthy connection where both feel safe.

It's important you learn that panic attacks, no matter how frightening the sufferer or those around them find, are not essentially dangerous. However, not all panic attacks present the same person-to-person. One individual could have the more classic "I feel like I am having a heart attack!" and be afraid of dying, while another feels a sudden disconnect from whatever is going on around them. People experiencing the former will often describe the feeling as somehow being outside of themselves or that they might even be going crazy, while the former may be rushed to the emergency room only to find there is nothing wrong with their heart. These frequently leave people feeling either misunderstood or like an idiot.

The aftereffects of such attacks can lead to continued tension in the person, and they may become overly sensitive to the way others respond or act around them. I'm not asking you to walk on eggshells, but being a calm and kind presence will go a long way to helping the sufferer of these attacks to settle down and have a clearer mind to be better able to process the circumstances that lead to the incident.

To learn more about the science behind how a panic attack can begin and the cascade that results from it, be sure to read Perkin's article to gain a better understanding. It is tempting to brush these off as someone just attention seeking, but this is not the case in someone having a panic attack. Panic attacks are very real and can have incredibly scary symptoms for the one experiencing them. Thankfully, though they tend to come on quite quickly, they also can subside rapidly as well. Usually in about 10 to 15 minutes.

The best thing you can do for your loved one is to remain calm and ask them if they have any pressure in their chest or pain radiating from their jaw or arm. If neither of these symptoms is present, you can reassure them everything is alright and to take slow breaths to match your own. If the sufferer states they have any of those symptoms, call for emergency assistance immediately. Even if for any reason you are unsure it's a panic attack, reach out to emergency services and let them do the assuring should there be no other medical issue occurring to cause the attack.

Multiple other symptoms can occur during a panic attack, so if you find yourself unsure what it is you are dealing with, again, remain calm and seek emergency help. If you are certain they are safe, you can try calling their doctor's office. Do not be surprised, however, if they suggest you still take them to the hospital just to be on the safe side. If something more serious is occurring, you might save a life.

If not, then you can use the opportunity to help the one suffering this anxious moment know they are safe and that you are someone that will treat them with dignity and respect. Do not belittle them. If they state they feel stupid, assure them they are not. What they experienced is very well and has a scientific basis and history. Thankfully, there are methods to help avoid future ones; one of the most important is allowing them to see the good that is in their lives, no matter how small.

TAKE STOCK OF YOUR OWN MENTAL STATE

Nothing begets more anxiety than being yelled at or even ignored when it feels like you cannot even trust what your body is telling you. You are already in fight-or-flight mode, and to top it all off, this is likely when you learn who really cares about you and who were "tissue-paper" friends. So, you must ask yourself this: Are you really there through thick and thin or only when you have something to gain from it?

Just because someone you know, be it a family member, a friend, or even a spouse, has been struggling with anxiety does not mean you are better than them. You, yourself, could be experiencing similar issues, and instead of looking to overcome your own trials, you are using another human being who is struggling as a way to make yourself feel superior. Anyone who bullies or cuts off someone simply because they get overly anxious or even has severe panic attacks without first trying to make a positive difference really should be taking a good look at themselves. Learn how to be more thoughtful and grateful to the people around you.

BE THE HOPE

You might have started reading this book to help someone else out, and that is pretty awesome. But, just as I've told everyone else reading this book, not even you can change another person. You can only change yourself. It would behoove you to apply the suggestions given in this book to yourself before trying to get another to do the same. Because, if there was any single thing you could do that would initiate positive change in anyone else around you, it would be that you already started the process within yourself. And that shines like a beacon of hope. So, be the hope.

CONCLUSION: LIFE GOES ON

Let me tell you how my week went. While the previous week had me feeling good, accomplished, and even on top of the world—mostly—I was unable to maintain that momentum into the next week. Each morning of the past week, I woke up motivated, even determined, to knock out my goals.

I always start with a bottle of water, ease into my favorite way to drink my coffee, spend some time reading my Bible, and then go for a run. When it comes to my choice in studying the Bible, I want to make it clear it could be any spiritual practice. You can choose to focus on Bible studies, breathing exercises, yoga nidra, meditation, even reading the Quran, and so on. I am not here to judge what people read; it's really about doing an engaging and enriching activity that empowers you enough that it takes you to your happy place.

Sadly, in my mind, at least, when it comes to me going for a run, it is mostly a fast walk as I attempt to get back into shape again. Still, managing to get that in several days a week makes me feel accomplished, and that is what I try to focus on the most. That

I tied my running shoes and put my foot on the treadmill, even if only for one mile.

After going through my list of things I wanted to get done first, such as my study and exercise, my next daily goal was to get in some writing for this book. To say I was easily distracted from writing last week would be an understatement. I discovered something interesting, though. While I had made time for you, my reader, to be prepared for some difficult and possibly triggering content, I forgot to ensure I did the same for myself.

Writing about my personal struggles as well as sharing the struggles of others with a similar history was taking a toll on me. I did not even realize it. I just wanted to do a good job, help others, and get my book written in a timely manner. Because I did not reach my word count goal last week, I started berating myself more and more as each day passed.

Saturday came, and because it's a day I always rest and refresh myself, I did not do any writing. Still, I allowed the tension of the work week to continue to brew quietly in the background. Saturday itself was actually a good day. However, it is only after I've had some time to think and refresh myself that I am most likely to have a strong negative reaction to something I might usually think little about. And Sunday was the proving ground of what happens when I forget to focus on what I do have and allow what I don't have to percolate in the back of my mind until it boils over. I fell apart completely and found myself crying and yelling at my husband when he had done nothing wrong.

Yes, I, the writer, fell apart under the weight of self-inflicted anxiety. You may wonder why I would admit to such a thing, but I would be completely remiss in leading you to believe I always have it together. Just because I've gotten help and made great progress does not mean those old demons of mine cannot flit around in the back of my mind.

They can be quietly insidious if I try to ignore their existence and not face them. The more I try to distract myself from them, the more they hook into me. They simply won't let go easily. It's like those darn hitchhikers you get when walking through a field. Or your overgrown backyard. Do not get me started about overgrown backyards. It's been that kind of week.

I comfort myself with the thought that even the most put-together person I know has bad, even terrible, days. Sometimes, bad weeks. This is why I am covering this subject here in this closing chapter. Nobody has a perfect life. And those who have suffered from anxiety, no matter the cause, are simply going to be more sensitive to stress. So, what can you do about those days when it all comes crashing down? You take care of yourself.

PUTTING IT ALL TOGETHER

Not everyone wants to try and find all the suggestions peppered throughout this book later on when they cannot recall the details. This is why I am putting it all together here in this last section. One of the easiest methods of refreshing your mind is to simply read over the contents outline. It's amazing how a few words can light up a corner of your mind to help bring something to light that will help you.

First things first: Remember, you are not alone. You are not weird or crazy, even though you may feel like you are. And don't tell me, "I like weird!" I like weird too but not the kind of weird that keeps us isolated from the people we care about the most. That is the problem with the word "weird." It has multiple connotations. Either way, I want you to understand there really is a medical and scientific reason for the way you feel.

And because there is a science to it, it means you have tools at your disposal to mix yourself with a better perspective by continuing to use tools that have proven to help. Just as shame and anxiety can feed off themselves, so can finding things to be grateful and delighted over that you have in your life. Building yourself and the life you live from the perspective of gratitude will take you far. The trick is making time to get in more of the things that cultivate a heart of gratitude.

If you struggle with this, don't forget you can always ask for help. You can talk to a trusted friend or relative or even your spouse. If you feel better talking to someone not so close to home, you can use the resources in Chapter 5 about CBT and ACT. Never be afraid to seek assistance either via personal contacts or by getting with a professional that can help you grow your gratitude and handle any anxiety you have positively.

If you have been engaged in a toxic relationship, know there is always help for that as well. Depending on the severity, you might have to remove yourself from the situation. If you've found there are things you can work on to improve yourself and your interaction with others, then take action. While you can only change yourself for the better and not anyone else, you can certainly influence them in a similar direction. Just as someone acting in negative ways can influence you to begin to take on their poor attributes.

This brings us to those who are reading in an effort to help a loved one. Be sure that your own actions and reactions reflect the sort of behavior you want to see in your loved one. So long as your motives are to help and grow closer to the person in a positive manner, you should be pleasantly surprised by what happens over time. It's not a quick fix, mind you, but persistence in adhering to your own gratitude and self-control does tend to eventually bring out the same in others.

WHAT YOU GET TO HAVE

I want you to make a promise to yourself. I do not care who you are or the reason why you read this book. I want you to promise to take good care of yourself. Your body, your mind, and even your spirituality.

Take a bubble bath, or spend time giving yourself a facial. I don't care if you are a man or a woman; washing your face with cool water has a calming effect. Self-care can be getting a massage or going for a walk in the sunlight. Or under the stars. Whatever floats your boat, do something that helps you appreciate even the little things.

We've talked about gratitude repeatedly, and it will be the rough times when it will shine the most. On those days when you realize you've been quietly shoving something onto the back-burner, and it's boiled over, understand what has happened and remind yourself of the things you get to have. I like phrasing it that way: "The things I get to have" are myriad, and I bet you get to have more than you realize.

I won't say you will always have control over your emotions and reactions. Even the most stoic of people can lose their cool. There may even be times you need to apologize and make amends for something you said or did during a strong emotional reaction. Not gonna lie, I've had to do that for my husband way too many times over the years. I am grateful—there it is!—for his calm during my storms.

It is because he started building his own gratitude after watching me struggle to do the same that our marriage survived. It makes me want to be the best version of myself I can be. It also encourages me that I am going to be okay. And so will you once you see everything you get to have all around you.

REFERENCES

Anxiety and Depression Association of America. (1979). *Personal stories.* https://adaa.org/educational-resources/from-our-community/stories-of-triumph

Anxiety and Depression Association of America. (2020). *Facts & statistics.* https://adaa.org/understanding-anxiety/facts-statistics#Facts%20and%20Statistics

Alzheimer's Association. (2019). *Caregiving.* https://www.alz.org/help-support/caregiving

Andrews, R. (2017, April 20). *This is what happens to your dog when you leave it alone.* IFLScience. https://www.iflscience.com/this-is-what-happens-to-your-dog-when-you-leave-it-alone-41328

Baton Rouge Behavioral Hospital. (2021, October 21). *Fear vs anxiety: Understanding the difference.* https://batonrougebehavioral.com/fear-vs-anxiety-understanding-the-difference/

Brulazzo, A. (2022). *Acceptance and commitment therapy: How to overcome traumas, anxiety and negative thoughts that depress your life through mindful change and self-compassion.* Independently published.

Cal y Mayor Galindo, P. (2021, April 30). *What is gratitude? 5 ways to be thankful.* BetterUp. https://www.betterup.com/blog/gratitude-definition-how-to-practice

Calm. (2019). *Experience calm.* https://www.calm.com/

Cirino, E. (2018, May 24). *10 tips to help you stop ruminating.* Healthline. https://www.healthline.com/health/how-to-stop-ruminating

REFERENCES

Clarke, S. (2017, November 11). *Anxiety success stories that will give you hope and inspiration.* ProjectEnergise.com. https://projectenergise.com/anxiety-success-stories/

Emily, M. (2021, September 27). *How growing up with alcoholic parents affects children.* Addiction Center. https://www.addictioncenter.com/alcohol/growing-up-alcoholic-parents-affects-children/

Gault, A. M. (2021, October 26). *How mindfulness meditation helped me find happiness in myself, for myself.* PSYCOM. https://www.psycom.net/yael-shy-mindfulness-meditation

Hassine, S. B. (2018). *The fabulous* [Mobile]. https://www.thefabulous.co/

Heshmat, S. (2019, August 25). *Music, emotion, and well-being.* Psychology Today. https://www.psychologytoday.com/us/blog/science-choice/201908/music-emotion-and-well-being

Hwang, W. (2022, January 3). *How to ruminate productively.* Psychology Today. https://www.psychologytoday.com/us/blog/flex-your-feelings/202201/how-ruminate-productively

Jauwena, G. (2019, February 26). *How to stop stress eating for good.* Life & Health Network. https://lifeandhealth.org/lifestyle/how-to-stop-stress-eating-for-good/0814489.html

Johnson, A. (2015, February 18). *This list of 50 low-cost hobbies will excite you.* Lifehack. https://www.lifehack.org/articles/money/this-list-50-low-cost-hobbies-will-excite-you-2.html

Junger, G. (Director). (1999). *10 things I hate about you* [Film]. Touchstone Pictures, Polaris Pictures, Mad Chance, Intandem Films.

Kablam Games. (2019). *Shop Titans* (11.0.2) [Mobile]. https://playshoptitans.com/

Layton, J. (2008, June 30). *Can piranhas really strip a cow to the bone in under a minute?* HowStuffWorks. https://animals.howstuffworks.com/animal-facts/piranha-eat-cows.htm

Mayo Clinic. (2018, May 4). *Anxiety disorders - Symptoms and causes.* https://www.mayoclinic.org/diseases-conditions/anxiety/symptoms-causes/syc-20350961

Mayo Clinic. (2019, March 16). *Cognitive behavioral therapy.* https://www.mayoclinic.org/tests-procedures/cognitive-behavioral-therapy/about/pac-20384610

Melody Beattie. (2021, December 3). *Gratitude.* https://melodybeattie.com/gratitude-2/

Merriam-Webster. (n.d.-a). *Agoraphobic.* https://www.merriam-webster.com/dictionary/agoraphobic

Merriam-Webster. (n.d.-b). *Cognitive behavioral therapy.* https://www.merriam-webster.com/dictionary/cognitive%20behavioral%20therapy

Merriam-Webster. (n.d.-c). *Dopamine.* https://www.merriam-webster.com/dictionary/dopamine

Merriam-Webster. (n.d.-d). *Fortitude.* https://www.merriam-webster.com/dictionary/fortitude

Merriam-Webster. (n.d.-e). *Gaslighting.* https://www.merriam-webster.com/dictionary/gaslighting

Merriam-Webster. (n.d.-f). *Gratitude.* https://www.merriam-webster.com/dictionary/gratitude

Merriam-Webster. (n.d.-g). *On "doomsurfing" and "doomscrolling."* https://www.merriam-webster.com/words-at-play/doomsurfing-doomscrolling-words-were-watching

Merriam-Webster. (n.d.-h). *Ruminate.* https://www.merriam-webster.com/dictionary/ruminate

Mind. (2018, July). *About anger.* https://www.mind.org.uk/information-support/types-of-mental-health-problems/anger/about-anger/

Muccino, G. (Director). (2006). *The pursuit of happyness* [Film]. Sony Pictures.

National Domestic Violence Hotline. (2018, October 8). *The national domestic violence hotline.* https://www.thehotline.org/

Perkins, C. (2021, August 4). *The science behind panic attacks — And what you can do to manage them.* TED. https://ideas.ted.com/the-science-behind-panic-attacks-and-what-can-you-do-to-manage-them

Peterson, J. B. (2018). *12 rules for life: An antidote to chaos.* Vintage Canada.

San Diego Zoo Wildlife Alliance. (2020). *Koi.* https://animals.sandiegozoo.org/animals/koi

Scott, E. (2022, April 4). *Top tips for relaxing your body and mind.* Verywell Mind. https://www.verywellmind.com/how-to-relax-physically-and-emotionally-3144472

Senior Lifestyle. (2020, October 2). *50 essential dementia resources for caregivers.* https://www.seniorlifestyle.com/resources/blog/50-essential-dementia-resources/

Stosny, S. (2014, October 18). *The fear-shame dynamic.* Psychology Today. https://www.psychologytoday.com/us/blog/anger-in-the-age-entitlement/201410/the-fear-shame-dynamic

Summer, J. (2021, June 23). *What are hypnopompic hallucinations?* Sleep Foundation. https://www.sleepfoundation.org/how-sleep-works/hypnopompic-hallucinations

The Hope for Depression Research Foundation. (2013). *Facts about depression.* https://www.hopefordepression.org/depression-facts/

Think Mental Health. (2017, October 21). *Maintaining mental health and wellbeing.* https://www.thinkmentalhealthwa.com.au/about-mental-health-wellbeing/ ways-to-look-after-your-mental-health/maintaining-mental-health-and-wellbeing/

Tzeses, J. (2021, November 9). *Why pursuing happiness makes us miserable.* PSYCOM. https://www.psycom.net/why-pursuing-happiness-makes-us-miserable

Vigo, A. (2022). *Make peace with anxiety.* Be Well Publisher.

ABOUT THE AUTHOR

Jennifer Kyndnes – suffers from anxiety and knows what it is like to battle her own demons. Anxiety had become part of her repertoire, and she could not engage in most activities without having the 'worried- response'. This book details how she went from anxiety to self-love: one step at a time, taking responsibility for herself and for the consequences of the choices she made, finally realizing self-love and being kind to yourself was the missing link to her overall wellbeing.

www.ingramcontent.com/pod-product-compliance
Lightning Source LLC
Chambersburg PA
CBHW062001040426
42447CB00010B/1846